Journal of Pren Perinatal Psycholog

Volume 13, Number 3–4, Spring & Summer 1999

CONTENTS

JOURNAL OF PRENATAL AND PERINATAL PSYCHOLOGY AND HEALTH publishes findings from the cutting edge of the rapidly growing science of pre- and perinatal psychology. The journal is the first periodical dedicated to the in-depth exploration of the psychological dimension of human reproduction and pregnancy and the mental and emotional development of the unborn and newborn child. It is intended to provide a forum for the many disciplines involved such as obstetrics, midwifery, nursing, perinatology, pediatrics, prenatal preparation, psychology, psychiatry, law, and ethology. The journal also deals with the numerous ethical and legal dilemmas which are emerging as society re-evaluates its attitudes toward adoption and abortion or strives to establish moral positions on high-tech obstetrics and third-party conception. The opinions expressed in articles and claims made in advertisements are those of the authors and advertisers, respectively, and do not imply endorsements by APPPAH or Allen Press, Inc.

MANUSCRIPTS should be submitted to the Editor, Ruth J. Carter, Ph.D., CBX 018, Georgia College, Milledgeville, Georgia 31061. The journal accepts only original material which is not under consideration by any other publication and which may not be reprinted without the consent of both author and Editor. The Editor reserves the right to edit manuscripts for length, clarity, and conformity with the journal's style. See inside back cover for style requirements.

SUBSCRIPTION inquiries and subscription orders should be addressed to the publisher at Subscription Department, APPPAH, 340 Colony Road, Box 994, Geyserville, CA 95441-0994 U.S.A. Subscription rates:

Volume 12, 1997–1998 (4 issues) $200.00 (outside the U.S., $220.00). Price for individual subscribers certifying that the journal is for their personal use, $50.00 (outside the U.S., $60.00).

INDEXED IN: APA Psychological Abstracts, Child Development Abstracts, Health Instrument File, Pastoral Care and Counseling Abstracts.

PHOTOCOPYING: Authorization to photocopy items for internal or personal use of specific clients is granted by APPPAH for users registered with the Copyright Clearance Center (CCC) Transactional Reporting Service, provided that the flat fee of $12.50 per copy per article (no additional per-page fees) is paid directly to the Copyright Clearance Center, Inc., 222 Rosewood Drive, Danvers, Massachusetts 01923. For those organizations which have been granted a photocopy license from CCC, a separate system of payment has been arranged. The fee code for users of the Transactional Reporting Service is 0883-3095/97 $12.50

ISSN 1097-8003   *JOPPPAH* **13(3–4) 187–318 (1999)**

Journal of Prenatal and Perinatal Psychology and Health, 13(3–4), Spring/Summer 1999

Editorial

The May 1999 issue of the *Ladies Home Journal* featured a cover story on the McCaughey septuplets. Much of the article continued to praise the undoubtedly well meaning and obviously devoted parents. Yet even the "cream puff" journalism of this ladies magazine eventually addressed the serious problems most of these seven small children suffer. The litany of difficulties include eye surgery for one and glasses for another. One boy was barely sitting up at his developmental first birthday. Two of the girls have severe reflux and have had more trauma inflicted upon them with esophageal surgery. Post-operatively, the children are still being fed through stomach tubes. The reporter commented in bemusement that both girls, "have so far managed to overcome medical science and the problem persists." One of these little girls also can not sit up and was described as being the size of a six month old infant.

During the same month a local Georgia newspaper headlined: *Court drops charges against women in fetal alcohol case—Fetus ruled not a human being.* The case involved a woman accused of trying to drink her fetus to death. The child survived but was born with a blood alcohol level of 0.199 percent, twice the level considered intoxicated under Wisconsin law where the case was tried. A mix-up in embryo implantation led to the birth of a black baby to white parents who surrendered the child to his genetic parents. Why are we not surprised that the custody exchange was described as "very emotional, very strained, very difficult"? The birth mother carried the child to term and cared for him for four months.

The enlightened treatment of birth trauma and the clarifying messages of pre- and perinatal psychology unfortunately still have not quite reached the hinterlands. Yet enormous progress has been made, largely due to the pioneers in this field several of whom are featured in this double issue of the *Journal.* A reprint of a 1990 address *Finding Our Voice* by APPPAH founder Thomas Verny, MD, D Psych, FRCP(C) and an article by Shirley Ward, M.Ed., DipEd., *Birth Trauma in Infants and Children* offer observations into the history and progress of pre-and perinatal psychology. Two articles *The Biopsychosocial Transactional Model of Development: The Beginning of The Formation of An Emergent Sense of Self in the Newborn* and *The Effects of Domestic Abuse on the Unborn Child* (coauthored by Thomas Verny with two of his students, Donis Eichhorn, RN, Ph.D and Amy L. Gilliland, B.A.) give us glimpses into the thoughts of individuals who will help propel this work into the future. Another student Bobbi J. Lyman, M.A., who is a Ph.D. candidate at the Fielding Institute, explores *Antecedents to Somatoform Disorders: A Pre- and Perinatal Psychology Hypothesis*. Mac Freeman, Ph.D., in *Before I Am, We Are*, brings charming wisdom to his concept of the "duet" of mother and child—before and after birth, while music therapist, Giselle E. Whitwell, R.M.T. echoes and embellishes this idea in her article *The Importance of Prenatal Sound and Music*. Millicent Adams Dosh, MA, suggests in *Prenatal and Perinatal Foundations of Moral Development* that solutions to aberrant behavior may be found in viewing "moral development on a continuum, from conception through death." Christine Caldwell, Ph.D., LPC, ADTR write in *Dying To Be Born, and Being Born To Die: Cell Death As a Defining Pattern In Human Development and Death:*

> One of natures most elegant synchronies occurs at the doorway of our two greatest life transitions—birth and death. they both involve a cessation of self the way we have known it and a journey into the unknown. Both involve cataclysmic physiological changes that permanently alter us.

Joann O'Leary, MS, MPH and Cecilie Gaziano, PhD, MA, present their research on *The Role of Childhood Memory Scores in Parenting in Pregnancy and Early Postpartum*. Their conclusions indicate that, "as expectant parents begin the developmental tasks of pregnancy, their own histories begin to resurface, consciously or subconsciously."

The Board of Directors of APPPAH invites you to attend the 9th International Congress of the organization from December 3–6, 1999 at the Cathedral Hill Hotel in San Francisco. The conference theme is *Birth and Consciousness in the New Millennium*. Pre Conference Workshops on December 2 and 3 include opportunities with Judith O. Weaver, Terry Levy, Bob Mandel, Aletha Solter and Gay and Katheryn Hendricks. Post Conference Workshops on December 7, include offerings by Joseph Chilton Pearce, Jeannine Parvati Baker, Peter Levine, Ray Castellino, Jon Turner and Isabella Barajon. The theme of the Congress seems to have been inspired by Shakespeare's well known and wonderful line from *The Tempest, O brave new world that hath such people in it.*

Ruth J. Carter, Ph.D.
Editor-in-Chief
Georgia College and State University
Milledgeville, Georgia

Journal of Prenatal and Perinatal Psychology and Health, 13(3–4), Spring/Summer 1999

LOOKING BACK
Finding Our Voice

Thomas Verny, M.D., D. Psych., F.R.C.P. (C)

You have all learned by now that this is not an Association for the faint of heart. There are millions of people in the world who are blind to the abuse of children and adults, who are blind to the environmental destruction of this planet and who are blind to the threat of nuclear annihilation. They lack any insight. They walk about in a state of unconsciousness. They are people whose psyches have become frozen from too much pain. They are either content or resigned to their lives.

There is a great gulf between us and them. We are wanderers, dreamers and searchers. We have not given up hope, we believe in the perfectibility of human nature and we believe that this can be achieved in humane and psychologically sound ways today.

Our focus is the study of the fundamental mysteries of the mind: when does life begin, how much and in what ways is an unborn child influenced by his or her environment, are a person's basic character traits formed before, during or after birth?

Just as Melville's *Moby Dick* can be read simply as an account of a whaling expedition, or read on a deeper allegorical level, the subject of pre- and perinatal psychology also lends itself to deeper explorations. The subtext deals with such questions as: what is the nature of reality? How do we arrive at knowledge? What is healing? This becomes clear when you study the writings and talk to some of the founders of pre- and perinatal psychology such as Otto Rank, Nandor Fodor, Francis Mott, Lietaert Peerbolte, Stanislav Grof, David Chamberlain, Michel Odent and others. As a result of their work they all underwent a major paradigm shift moving from a strictly mechanistic-scientific world view to a much more spiritual-humanistic world view.

This paper is an excerpt from the Presidential Address by APPPAH founder, Thomas Verny, at the 4th international congress of the Association in Amherst, Massachusetts. It is reprinted from our *Journal,* volume 4 (3), 1990.

Let me give you some examples to illustrate these points. This is from a paper written by Averil Earnshaw, an Australian child psychiatrist describing her experiences in a London, England children's ward: (Journal of Child Psychology Vol. 7, No. 2; 1981) Baby X was lying in his container, watched by his special nurse; he was a wrinkled little fellow weighing just over two pounds, and he had many connections. An intravenous drip tube ran into his umbilical cord, one tube disappeared into each nostril, (one to his stomach and one to his duodenum), and he had an in-dwelling rectal lead measuring his temperature. Because he was a lively, wriggly fellow, and tended to brush at his tubes, and to displace them, his hands had been "gloved" and tied loosely down.

As we watched him, his mouth opened and began to seek, I thought. His head moved from side to side a little, mouthing and gasping. He pulled with his arms against the ties, and his mouthing turned to grimacing. His breathing was becoming faster and faster and he seemed more and more distressed, till suddenly it stopped. He exhaled all his carbon dioxide, which is the body's main chemical stimulus to respiration.

As he became gradually blue and floppy, his nurse became pale and frantic-holding a tiny oxygen mask over his face. We both thought he might not breathe again—but he did—and recovered his color. By this time the nurse was pale and sweating and we were both feeling shaken. As the nurse and I shared our anxiety, I commented on my impression that the baby got so upset when he wanted something in his mouth, and that I had seen similar episodes before.

Soon the baby began to stir again, to wriggle and then to mouth blindly, and to breathe fast again. I slipped the tip of my little finger in his mouth and he latched on tightly and began to suck strongly, now breathing quite regularly. One blue eye looked at us, then the other, and nurse cried out "he's never opened his eyes before!" After a minute or so, he closed his eyes and his gums loosened on my finger and I then removed it.

"If he asks again," I said to nurse, "you give him your finger; he's really strong." When the cycle began again, nurse did offer her finger; she was uncertain but felt it might be the lesser of two evils—the risk of a "non-sterile" finger, as she said, or the risk of another episode of cyanosis and collapse. The baby sucked strongly and once again opened his eyes to gaze at her as he sucked. "But they can't suck!" said the nurse "the book says so."

The following is a brief example from R. D. Laing's autobiography *Wisdom, Madness, and Folly* (New York: McGraw-Hill, 1985).

In a recent seminar that I gave to a group of psychoanalysts, my audience became progressively aghast when I said that I might accept a cigarette from a patient without making an interpretation. I might even offer a patient a cigarette. I might even give him or her a light. And what if a patient asked you for a glass of water? one of them asked almost breathlessly. "I would give him or her a glass of water and sit down in my chair again," he said. Would you not make an interpretation?, she asked. "Very probably not," he replied. A lady exclaimed, "I'm totally lost!"

My last example appeared in *Medical News,* March 3, 1986:

In a remarkable study that was both double blind and randomized, cardiologist Randy Byrd, arranged for prayer groups to pray for half of the 393 patients in a San Francisco coronary care unit. Those prayed for and those not prayed for were comparable in terms of age and severity of medical condition.

The prayers—Protestants, Catholics, and Jews who lived in parts of California, Oregon, and the East Coast—were given the names of the patients, their diagnoses, and their condition. They were asked to pray *every day* in any way they chose, and to include a prayer for "beneficial healing and quick recovery." Patients in the study groups each had five to seven people praying for them, either gathered in prayer groups or, most often, praying individually.

The outcomes indicated that the recipients of prayer improved more and had fewer complications than did the control group. Only three in the experimental group required antibiotics, compared with 16 of those in the control group. Only six who were prayed for experienced pulmonary edema (water logging of the lungs), compared with 18 controls. None of the experimental group required intubation, compared with 12 in the control group.

What are we to make of this? Are you going to shrug it off as nonsense, will you consider it for a few months and then forget about it? Will you accept it in its totality? As you think about these questions, you are struggling with complex issues such as what information do you trust? Do you trust your own experience, your intuition, experts, or textbooks? How do you discover and then break out of self-imposed limiting belief systems?

When I went to medical school I was taught: "once a C-section always a C-section;" "malnutrition spares the brain," "the placental barrier protects a baby from toxins," and "thalidomide is a safe drug for pregnant women" et cetera.

All of these obstetrical homilies have been shown to be totally erroneous. But there are others which still persist; e.g., "the fetus and the neonate feel no pain and even if they did, they would forget it." How is it that neonatal anesthesiologists believe that premature and newborn babies cannot feel pain? How are they able to look at writhing, screaming infants and not be touched by their agony? Helen Harrison, a mother, was one of the first to react publicly about her baby's surgery without anesthesia (*Birth*, 13(2), 124, 1986).

"Ten years ago our prematurely born son, Edward, was shunted for hydrocephalus while paralyzed with curare. Although he could not move, cry, or react in any way, he could see, hear, and feel as large incisions were cut in his scalp, neck, and abdomen. A hole was drilled in his skull; a tube was inserted into the center of his brain and pushed down under the skin of his neck, chest, and abdomen and implanted deep in his abdominal cavity. It is a source of great anguish to me that my husband and I signed a form allowing such an operation to take place, but we were told Edward might die or become brain damaged without the operation and that anesthesia might kill him. "Besides," the doctors assured us, "these babies don't really feel pain." I suspected then, and now know, that this is just not true."

"To this day, our severely retarded son will allow no one to touch his head, neck or abdomen. Even heavily tranquilized, he reacts to the medical procedures or the mere sight of the hospital with violent trembling, profuse sweating, screaming, struggling, and vomiting. I can't help feeling that on some level he still remembers the hideous pain inflicted on him during his unanesthetized surgery and throughout the course of his neonatal intensive care."

"At the 1985 national conference of Parents of Premature and High Risk Infants, I joined a group of mothers and fathers who were discussing their children's painful NICU care: major surgery, chest tube insertions, cut-downs (all performed without painkillers) gangrene and amputations from infiltrated IVs; bones broken during chest physiotherapy; skin pulled off with adhesive tape; burns from the monitors; 24-hour-a-day bombardment with bright light and loud noise; and numerous iatrogenic afflictions from improperly evaluated therapies. "If this were going on in any other setting," one mother exclaimed, "it would be called torture!" Another added that if these procedures were carried out on kittens and puppies instead of human babies, anti-vivisectionists would close down the nurseries."

In contrast, it gives me great personal satisfaction that at this congress we are holding major symposia on pain in the perinatal period, and the effect of sensory bombardment on neonates in NICUs. I think it is high time that we let the world know that this Association and the people of this nation are committed to the eradication of child abuse in all its forms whether it be sexual, physical, mental or medical.

RESISTANCE TO APPPAH

Resistance to pre- and perinatal psychology is widespread, tenacious, and takes many forms. I shall discuss briefly four identifiable groups from which you may expect criticism:

Feminist Foes

In November 1987 1 wrote a letter to Michele Landsberg, wife of Stephen Lewis, then Canada's Ambassador to the United Nations. I asked her to support our plan to hold an international conference under United Nations auspices sometime in the future and to name that year "The Year of the Pregnant Parent." I gave her a history of our Association and described its aims. Here are two paragraphs from her four paragraph response:

"For me, this issue is intimately and indissolubly linked to the welfare of mothers. Reading your material, I was disturbed by the blurring out of the mother as a person, e.g. "The Rights of Pregnant Parents" (ever seen a pregnant father? Would women and children be the world's poorest citizens if men could get pregnant?) Furthermore, I cannot support any organization that is "non-political" on abortion. On an issue of such profound and intimate centrality to women's autonomy, there's no middle ground. To be non-political is not enough."

"Also, yet another organization in which predominantly male scientists are carrying on about "life beginning at conception" and arranging conferences, grants, power structures and publicity for themselves, in the course of which they will pronounce about the rights and wrongs of reproductive technologies which prey on women, seems to me misguided. Feminists have learned the hard way to distrust doctors and scientists who continually seek to take over and control (through gynecology, obstetrics, reproductive technology, psychiatry) women's lives."

The most common objection from women that I have heard about my book, *The Secret Life of the Unborn Child* has been: Now we have something more to feel guilty about!" or "Here is another man telling us what we have done wrong." Related to this is the view amongst some women that pregnancy limits their God-given freedom to do with their bodies as they like even if that includes the ingestion or inhalation of toxic substances clearly demonstrated to be harmful to their babies.

Right Wing Reactionaries

These individuals despise anyone and any philosophy that advocates the treatment of people with feeling and respect—even babies. They portray us as "flaky," and quite divorced from the real world, a world which only they understand.

The following is from an article by Joanne Jacobs in the Santa Barbara News-Press, 1987:

> "Nowadays, you can ruin your child's life before he's even born," my pregnant sister announced after reading a book called *The Secret Life of the Unborn Child.* Joanne was skeptical. "I always thought you had to wait till the kid was born." The kid is born now and has lots of silky black hair, and the big cheeks and receding chin of the classic baby. According to the unborn child psychology movement, he is ruined, damaged goods, doomed to low self-esteem and a future of violence, criminality, perversion and Republicanism. This is nonsense, but it's dangerous nonsense.

As this child was being born on July 10, the 3rd International Congress of Pre- and Perinatal Psychology was meeting in San Francisco to discuss birthing better babies. Calling us "new age" unborn child psychologists, our opponents caricature our view that "everything" a woman thinks, says, feels and hopes—from the moment of conception to the moment of birth—influences the unborn child. They ridicule the idea there is a "perfect" way to be pregnant, to give birth, and to "bond" after birth. If parents do it right they will create an ideal child, and if they do it wrong, they'll get Boy George.

The Gods of Science

Scientists suffer from the same foibles and prejudices as all of us do, perhaps more so. Our minds tend to cling to the familiar and to defend against the unfamiliar. Naturally, the more you have invested in the status quo the more you will resist questioning your established ideas and values. The leaders of the scientific community have spent many years of sweat and tears to achieve their present positions of prestige and financial security. Any notion or research finding which could prove their life-long beliefs wrong is incredibly threatening to them.

Furthermore, scientists, academics and health professionals like the rest of us, live with varying degrees of residual pre- and peri-natal trauma. Any talk about babies being sensate and sensible beings triggers their unconscious pain. And they defend against this with denial and hostility. Sometimes their attacks will take the high road, sometimes the low road. Whichever road they travel their criticism usually focuses on our lack of one or more of the following: proper scientific training, proper academic standing, or proper objectivity. We are just not very proper by their standards.

This proclivity to treat the proponents of unorthodox ideas as if they were misguided, retarded and naive is aggravated by the tendency of the media to equate scientific credibility with academic appointments. These defenders of the public good always feel it their duty to balance any story about pre- and peri-natal psychology with the obligatory quote from a "local authority." Sometimes this person may be a pediatrician friend of the journalist, or perhaps the head of obstetrics of the local hospital, or on a psychology faculty somewhere. These people, who have usually never even heard of our work, become instant experts as they caution the gullible public against being deceived by "unsubstantiated claims"—a favorite expression of our detractors.

Let me give you examples of this latter approach. In *Hippocrates,* July/August 1987, William Poole wrote an extensive article on Rene Van de Carr's Prenatal University. In the middle of an otherwise excellent article comes the requisite rebuttal to wit: "Michael Meyerhoff, associate director of the Center for Parent Education in Newton, Massachusetts, is another skeptic. 'People like to talk to a baby before it's born. It's a natural thing to do. We also talk to dogs and vending machines. But it's irresponsible for a professional to encourage talking to fetuses in this way.' "

I wonder if the reporter ever bothered to ask Michael Meyerhoff whether he was familiar with the latest research in the field of pre- and perinatal psychology? Does he subscribe to the *Pre and Perinatal Psychology Journal?* What gives him the right to denounce and ridicule persons whom he has never met and whose work he has not studied?

Just one more example to illustrate the patronizing tone so common among many local heroes. About a year ago I gave a talk in a small town in British Columbia. About two hundred people showed up including two family physicians. Following my presentation they both wrote critical letters to the editor of the town's newspaper. Here is a tiny excerpt from one of these letters:

A recent copy of a medical journal set out some standards for acceptance of an article. Certain factors are evident and common-sense: 1) Are the facts adequately referenced? 2) Are opinions substantiated? 3) If there is original research is the method clearly described, are results correct, discussion adequate, and conclusions justified? 4) If there are general conclusions of fact involved can the research be duplicated by other scientific workers? As it appears that Dr. Verny depends a great deal on anecdotal comments and on loose, vague generalizations, then it would appear that we are dealing with another of history's interesting but faddish temporary phenomena, akin perhaps to phrenology or mesmerism.

Wolves in Sheep's Clothing

In a sense, these people are the most difficult to deal with because they pretend to have adopted new attitudes when, in fact, it is the same old medical model dressed up to look like all the things pregnant women have been asking for. I think the following excerpt from an article in the *New York Times* November 13, 1988, will illustrate my point:

> "Natural childbirth is alive and well," said Dr. Maurice L. Druzin, director of obstetrics at New York Hospital-Cornell Medical Center, "but it has become a marriage of biology and technology." Although there are no reliable statistics on the use of painkillers and monitoring devices in delivery, doctors and other experts around the country agree that the definition of natural childbirth is changing to include any birth in which the mother is awake and delivers vaginally."

INSTITUTING SOCIAL CHANGES

We need to constantly remember that we are explorers of a new frontier. We are the trustees of a dream and a vision. We are engaged in a struggle for social change. Therefore, passivity is a luxury in which we cannot afford to indulge. We cannot sit back and hope that the *Truth* which to us is so evident will also be evident to Dr., Mr., or Ms. Public. It is incumbent upon us to bring the data, the theories, and the concepts of pre- and peri-natal psychology to their homes, offices, schools, hospitals and a million other places.

We can do so institutionally and personally. As an association we hold biennial international congresses, publish a quarterly journal and newsletter, and collaborate with other organizations. In January 1986 we arranged a very successful conference in Newport Beach, California in cooperation with the Institute for the Advancement of Human Behavior. We also have many speakers in our association who ceaselessly and fearlessly carry our message to the farthest corners of the world.

I do not think that we have been as successful on the personal, grass roots level as we have on the organizational level. It would be immensely helpful to our association if you started to talk to your friends and colleagues about joining the Association, promoting our journal to your local University or hospital library, started a regional study group, organized fund raisers, or invited one of our speakers to talk to your professional association (e.g., the Humanistic Psychology Association, NAPSAC, National Associations of Neonatal Nurses, etc.)

Believe me, I know well that engaging in "subversive" activities such as supporting APPPAH takes time, energy, money, and sometimes it even earns you disapproval from professional colleagues. But do you have a choice? If you are deeply concerned with the state of our hurting and endangered planet, then you must act with fierceness of heart and courage of spirit. I ask you to be radical in your humanism and passionate in the pursuit of the goals we have set forth in our Association.

You all know the saying "It's better to light a candle than to curse the darkness." For God's sake, let us light a whole bunch of candles so that we can begin to illuminate this country and beyond. And let us not wait until all the double blind studies are in, until the political climate is right, until the economy is right, until tomorrow or next year when you will have more time. Let us resolve, individually and collectively, that the time is right, the place is right, the time is now, and the place is here.

Journal of Prenatal and Perinatal Psychology and Health, 13(3–4), Spring/Summer 1999

Birth Trauma in Infants and Children

Shirley A. Ward, M.Ed. DipEd.

'Newborn babies have been trying for centuries to convince us they are, like the rest of us, sensing, feeling, thinking human beings.'
David Chamberlain PhD

Some years ago I received a phone call from the Gerry Ryan Show, on Irish National Radio, because they are aware of the Pre and Perinatal therapeutic work we do with adults and children at *Amethyst* (a Center of Resource for Human Development in Ireland). During the radio broadcast a distressed mother phoned in for help because her fourteen month old son screamed and cried in his sleep relentlessly and the family had not had a good night's sleep since he was born. Her concern was for her son and what could be causing his distress. I recognised that the symptoms were probably related to a birth trauma. I asked her what her son's birth had been like. She responded that she was in the hospital and she had been awake during the birth but that her son had the cord around his neck which had caused him, and her, great distress.

I suggested that the child's behavior was a possible birth trauma and there was a treatment developed by William Emerson called *Birth Simulating Massage* to treat infant birth trauma. The massage was something that she could do herself for her baby—and involved gentle stroking and holding patterns simulating pressures on the infant's body that were most traumatised during birth. Since her description

Shirley A. Ward M.Ed. DipEd., with founder Alison Hunter, is a director of Amethyst Resource Center for Human Development and International Advisor for APPPAH. She may be reached at 28 Beech Court, Killiney, County Dublin, Ireland.
Email: amethyst@iol.ie.
Website http://www.holistic.ie/amethyst
Author's note: Dr David Chamberlain, Dr Thomas Verny, Dr William Emerson and Dr Violet Oaklander are long standing Patrons and Friends of *Amethyst*. They are generous with their time and are available as consultants and advisors for the *Amethyst* therapists and students.

clearly indicated a cord trauma, I suggested that she hold her baby, love him, talk softly to him and then very gently massage his neck. His reaction would probably be to scream and cry if the distress was coming from the trauma of the cord around his neck. It was very important to affirm and love the baby in between the stroking and massaging. This treatment would help to desensitise the trauma that was still possibly causing his distress. Twenty four hours later she phoned me. Her son had reacted by screaming and crying as she intuitively stroked his neck. A week later she phoned again—the treatment had dramatically dissipated the symptoms, all was now peaceful and her baby son was no longer distressed—it had worked—they had all had the best night's sleep in fourteen months!

Time and time again we have feedback from parents when it has been suggested that some of their children's problems may be stemming from birth trauma. Much of it is positive. I remember over thirty years ago, as a teacher, I was very involved in teaching the children with behaviour, emotional and learning difficulties. Some mothers would comment that their child had a difficult birth and they were sure it had affected their son or daughter. How right they were—but it wasn't until I met Dr Frank Lake in the 1970's that I had any idea of the research and experiential work that was going on with adults, which was later to help infants and children.

A BRIEF HISTORY OF THE THEORY OF BIRTH TRAUMA

From the 1920's a number of European psychologists and clinicians wrote or researched the effects of prenatal and perinatal experiences on human growth and developmant. Various patterns of dysfunctional behaviour were found, relating to prenatal and birth trauma (Fodor 1949; Peerbolte, 1975; Lake, 1966; Laing, 1977).

Some of the first indications that babies are conscious came from the pioneering work of Sigmund Freud and the practice of psychoanalysis going back to the beginning of the century. Freud was skeptical about how the infant mind worked, but client information seemed to link their anxieties and fears to events surrounding their births. Freud theorised that birth might be the original trauma upon which later anxiety was based.

When Freud's associate, Otto Rank, wrote *The Trauma of Birth* in 1923 it was inconceivable that research over the next seventy years would bring such an open window to the hidden world of the womb and substantiate Rank's ideas. As Frank Lake so aptly put it—"The Womb is a Room with a View."

Primal orientated treatment of pre and perinatal experiences with adults was being researched by Frank Lake in England from the late 1960's; in USA by Arthur Janov (1974), Leonard Orr (1977) and in USA and Europe by Stanislav Grof (1975). Frank Lake lectured and introduced his work to Ireland in the latter part of the 1970's and Alison Hunter ran workshops from 1978, founded *Amethyst* in 1982 and pioneered Lake's work in Ireland.

All of this research and development except for a minimum of exploratory investigation (Mott 1952) was directed towards adult patients.

PIONEERS IN BIRTH PSYCHOLOGY

In the mid 1970's and early 1980's it was time for the children to be considered—if birth trauma affects adults what are the odds that children are also affected and need help. A great deal of research has gone into finding evidence for the full range of infant capabilities, whether from personal reports contributed by parents, revelations arising from therapeutic work or from formal experiments.

Amongst the most outstanding researchers are Thomas Verny and David Chamberlain, both pioneers in birth psychology. They founded the Pre and Perinatal Psychology Association of North America (PPPANA) in 1983. It is now renamed The Association for Pre and Perinatal Psychology and Health (APPPAH). They and members of the Association are continuing to research the impacts of pre and perinatal experiences worldwide.

In 1981 Thomas Verny, the Canadian psychiatrist published his best selling book *The Secret Life of the Unborn Child* (now available in 25 languages) and in it he wrote:

> There is a growing body of empirical studies showing significant relationships between birth trauma and a number of specific difficulties; violence, criminal behaviour, learning disabilities, epilepsy, hyperactivity and child alcohol and drug abuse.

In 1988 David Chamberlain, an American psychologist practising in San Diego, California, published his groundbreaking book *Babies Remember Birth*. Also translated into many languages the book has been reprinted under the title *The Mind of Your Newborn Baby*. This extraordinary book takes you to the leading edge of scientific and medical research—providing scientific evidence proving that in the womb foetuses experience a wide variety of emotions; that the random noises newborns make are conscious attempts to communicate; and that cognition and reason in newborns are more highly developed than we previously believed.

TREATMENT FOR BIRTH TRAUMATISED CHILDREN

One of the leading researchers in the world for treatment with birth traumatised infants and children is Californian psychologist and psychotherapist, Dr William Emerson. He began the development and research for infants and children in 1974. In the autumn of 1976 he visited Frank Lake in England in order to study birth and prenatal phenomena with him. Emerson began to question whether infants and children would benefit from forms of treatment especially developed for them.

To try and evaluate this theory, Emerson conducted a series of parent-child workshops throughout Europe in the late 1970's and early 1980's with children ranging from three to thirteen. His main focus was to clarify ordinary or unusual difficulties the children were having, and to experimentally use birth discussions, music and birth games to ascertain possible traumatic antecedents.

The artwork, fanatasies and dreams of the children were also collected. A number of findings came from this work:

- Birth issues were rampant in the art, fantasies and dreams of the children, especially before the age of eight.
- Birth and play were temperamentally related; the moodier the child, the greater the likelihood that play would be birth orientated (eg. climbing through bars or tunnels, trapping each other under beds etc).
- The more severe the difficulties the children were having, the more intense and frequent were birth issues.
- Ninety five percent of the children were able to remember significant aspects of their births, and a majority of these were able to re-experience their particular trauma.
- In the latter cases especially, spontaneous changes in the presenting difficulties and other problems were quite common.

(Emerson 1984)

TREATMENT OF AN INFANT

William Emerson's treatment of infant trauma began in 1974 in London when parents of a severely birth traumatised infant, and their doctor, brought her along. She was suffering from severe respiration distress which later developed into infant asthma. She also had difficulty ingesting fluids of any kind and as well as an irregular sleep pattern, was experiencing weight loss.

Emerson treated the traumatised infant with his *Birth Simulating Massage*. To simulate pressures of the uterus and pelvis during birth, gentle massage is applied to the affected areas where there has been pressure on the infant's body during the birth process. These places can be automatically and spontaneously found as the baby reacts to certain areas that are massaged. The emotional work is largely complete when there is no emotional reaction to the simulated birth pressure.

In the infant, the symptoms were dramatically altered after two one-hour sessions and completely resolved after three. Asthmatic children are prone to a high incidence of bronchial, lung, ear, nose and throat symptoms. A fifteen year follow up of this child reported no further bronchial or asthmatic episodes, and very low incidents of coughs or colds.

As their emotional work is complete another phase begins which Emerson calls schematic repatterning. The movement patterns that babies use to get from the uterus to the outside world are deeply imbedded and retained in the nervous system and body. These movement patterns he calls birth schema, which may be referred to by others as life scripts, colouring of life patterns, learned responses or behaviour traits; they may be positive or dysfunctional in their impacts.

Emerson believes that dysfunctional birth schema form from highly frustrated and/or impotent movement patterns during birth and provide a predispositional basis for a variety of childhood syndromes. These include learning disabilities, conduct and anxiety disorders, hyperactivity, problems of socialisation and aggression. The research work of Verny and Chamberlain, and our experiences at *Amethyst* would certainly support Emerson's findings. The action patterns or response learned behaviour from traumatic births do change as these trauma dissipate during treatment.

How Can Parents Recognise Birth Trauma Related Problems in Their Children?

Parents bring children into treatment for birth trauma when they know their child had a difficult birth and when there may be disturbed behaviour relating to it—although until it is brought to their attention the parents may not have the knowledge that the two events may be related.

When parents hear that babies remember birth they may feel guilty—but there is no need for parental guilt. Often it is not the type of birth they themselves would have wanted for their baby. Sometimes they are caught up in the type of birth prevalent at the time. No mother or father wants a stressful pregnancy or traumatic birth but it can result from a number of factors like relationship difficulties, environmental problems, unemployment, ill health—all of which contribute to the pressures of life.

The type of behaviour parents may observe in their children related to birth trauma may be aggression, excessive anger, anxiety, nervousness, not relating to other siblings or parents, insecurity, hanging on or excessive pleasing, stuck in fears like sleeping in the dark, excessive screaming or crying, not eating well, weight loss, separation anxieties at being left at school.

Hyperactive children also need positive help. Tom was a hyperactive child and had a most erratic sleep pattern. His mother continued a very busy teaching job during the pregnancy—hardly having time for his birth before she went back to work. Tom's hyperactivity in the family with his siblings was almost impossible. When he was seven he was given a violin and at the age of ten was able to play five different musical instruments. Twenty years later he is a successful professional solo violinist. Hyperactive children are usually very creative and there are ways to channel the energy. When I was ten my own father gave me a hockey stick—which eventually channelled my energy into becoming a professional sportswoman!

The withdrawn child may need to retreat from a world which is too painful. The quiet or shy child may not be brought for help. They are often seen as *good* by parents, being well behaved and not troublesome. Violet Oaklander (1978) points out that the problem only becomes evident when the shy behaviour is exaggerated through the child hardly ever speaking, or whispering. They may become *loners,* have few friends and become the object of bullying.

BIRTH RELATED DIFFICULTIES

Each of our births is different which may in part be the reason why each of us is unique. There are many other birth issues but the following are brief and general guidelines. Medical classifications for birth trauma are breech, forceps, vacuum extraction, caesarian, anaesthesia and from research we would also add induction, premature and also late arrival babies (Ward 1991).

Early or premature babies may want to arrive early for everything and be anxious not to be late—but they may never feel ready for anything. They may react as though there is not enough time and may feel rushed by others, causing an irrational aggression. Parents may have difficulties if they try to push their children too soon to do things—the child may want to stand on the sidelines and watch.

Late or postmaturity babies may not want to take the initiative. They may get very anxious if they are late but will probably feel they are running out of time—but still leave things until the very last minute! It may take *late* babies a long time to get going and may perhaps be late developers and slow in learning. The greater frustration may be with the parents!

Caesarian section babies may sit back and wait for everything to be done for them. They lack self empowerment and self worth—being 'taken out' they did not have the vaginal struggle and feel they haven't done anything to deserve what they have. The parents of caesarian borns have the difficult task of teaching their children how to do things for themselves, and to teach them boundaries that they never had like vaginal borns. They will probably do the opposite to what you say! Help is seen as a put down or a disempowerment. There is also the possibility that parents may not be able to get them out of the house as they grow older—and they may need some physical assistance!

Anesthetised babies may blame parents for their inability to function. They may have difficulty taking responsibility for their own actions. When trying to relate with them you may experience a 'fading in and out'. They may have low energy, deaden their feelings and their contact and are often difficult to 'reach'. Their concentration can be seriously affected. There is an added observation from research that 'anaethetised' children as they get older may turn to drugs to 'escape from the pressures of life'. Another reason for turning to drugs may be to avoid pain—as their mothers did during labour.

Babies are induced due to lack of progression, when labour needs to be started for external reasons (eg contractions are not strong enough or the mother is ill). Induced children are usually very stubborn. They have problems getting started and will resent being told what to do; "wait—I'm not doing this until I am ready—then I'll do it my way". They may not see another person's point of view, may be quite contrary and say "No" to any suggestion.

Breech born babies are either born buttocks or feet first. This is a violent birth and the baby often develops into a victim. They cannot get things in order and others will wonder why they can't do things which seem quite natural to them. They will keep trying but seem to get nothing right. They may well be in conflict with themselves and parents and display disappointment to self and others. There is a tendency to passive anger and an inner violence.

Babies need forceps because they are stuck and cannot get out fast enough. This problem may be due to a large head, mother's small pelvis, insufficient contractions and a complicated presentation. The birth is violent—help comes at last but can that support ever be trusted again? They will start something but have difficulty finishing it because of all the obstructions or distractions on the way. They may appear to be cut off from their emotions and be shy and withdrawn, and be prone to headaches and nausea.

It is quite remarkable in a traumatic forceps birth which has developed into a body schema, that the child will reach a point of confusion in conversation. At this point the head shakes back and forth as the child is trying to wrestle free of the forceps and the current argument, his or her forceps/oppositional personality has got him or her into!

Bullying in Ireland is a behavioural problem affecting the lives of thousands of school children and their families. At primary school level over one in ten children are involved in bullying on a frequent basis. According to Dr Mora O'Moore (1994) one child in five is afraid to go to school because of the fear of being bullied. Bullying is the persistant, wilful, conscious desire to hurt another and put that person under stress. It is carried out through verbal, physical, gesture, exclusion and extortion bullying.

Children who bully have an aggressive attitude towards peers, parents and teachers. All aggressive actions come from fear and the child who bullies may have had an aggressive reaction to a traumatic birth with a real underlying fear of dying. If bullying is intentional to hurt others, it is possible that the bullying related to birth trauma might be unconscious revenge on the forceps.

The child who is bullied may have a passive reaction to a traumatic birth with a real fear of dying. The victim is often seen as different, may be hypersensitive, cautious, anxious, passive or submissive and is not determined, forceful or decisive.

A report published by the Charity Kidscape on 21st April 1998, found that children who were bullied at school are up to seven times more likely to try to kill themselves. More research is needed—even by schools to note down on children's record cards the type of birth they had and whether there is any correlation to behaviour patterns later.

A leading question is whether the type of birth trauma a child has leads to bullying, and also to types of suicide attempts. Research evidence shows for example the cord round the neck may lead to suicide by hanging; a drugged birth may lead to overdose and gas or anesthetic at birth may lead to death by car exhaust fumes in place of the gas oven asphyxiation of an earlier era.

WORK WITH INFANTS, CHILDREN AND TEENAGERS AT AMETHYST

Carmel Byrne and I work with infants, children and teenagers—and also teach parents, therapists and others the different techniques for birth trauma healing. They include play therapy, storytelling as in birth stories, animal stories to reach aggression, birth simulating massage, movement and mime, painting, art, toys, role play, sand trays, birth games, tents, caterpillar tunnels and cushions. The improvisation and restructuring of birth trauma with babies from six weeks old is done using gentle massage and music with energy healing work.

Carmel stresses that although children go into traumatised states they are provoked by play therapy, gently and in small groups. The parents are present if possible with other family members—brothers, sisters, grandparents. who may be instrumental to the success of the empathic process. There is immediate bonding with loving cuddles from the parents, often with soft music in the background.

WORKING WITH INDUCTION AND BREECH BIRTH TRAUMA

A distraught mother brought her eleven year old son to Carmel. The major problem was his fear of the dark. He was dyslexic and was never ready for anything whether he liked where he was going or not. Getting him ready for a party or school was impossible—he would play with the dog, his toys, his computer games or read a book.The mother knew his birth had been difficult. The baby was not ready to be born. The medical staff induced labor and the child was born breech.

The therapist prepared the room with toys, a child's tent and a caterpillar tunnel to be used to simulate the womb experience. The toy he chose was a large, brown, lanky monkey which could pass as the placenta—Michael said it was his monster.

He did understand he was reliving his birth. The room was darkened gradually by drawing the curtains and Michael played in his tent. He came out of the tent feet first always stating he was not ready and it wasn't the right way. This was helping him desensitise his breech birth and letting him do it in his own time.

In the sixth session he stated that however long it took he would do it his way. So he went into his tent and sat and sat. Suddenly he said "I'm ready now", "Is there anybody there at all"? There was silence as the therapist and mother listened to him. "Listen to me," he shouted and got into a terrible rage. Cushions were put at the end of the tunnel and Michael came out head first, doing it his way and empowering himself.

No more sessions were needed and his mother reported that Michael was studying better at school. He was no longer afraid of the dark and the constant struggle of not being on time had dissipated.

ENERGY HEALING WITH A BIRTH TRAUMATISED BABY WITH A HOLE IN THE HEART

Babies and children are very responsive to the use of energy healing within a play or therapy session. A single mother brought along her seven month old baby, Katy, because she had a hole in the heart which had developed at seven months in utero. The mother understood that Katy's birth had been difficult, with a long labour. Birth was a high forceps delivery, the baby was born purple with distress, was choking and had difficulty breathing. She was thought to be dying but she was resuscitated and put into intensive care.

During the second session of healing Katy turned purple, went very cold and her breathing became erratic. Her mother remarked that this was how her birth had been. Carmel held Katy's head very gently a birth trauma session developed involving gentle stroking to desensitise the trauma of the forceps.

The mother continued to bring Katy for healing for well over a year. At sixteen months of age Katy went for her medical check up and the hole in the heart was smaller. At eighteen months of age the hole in the heart had closed.

HEALING SEVERE BIRTH TRAUMA

Colette aged eighteen months, was brought by her parents to Carmel because she was crying excessively, was not sleeping day or night, and screamed in terror and rage if she was touched, particularly on the head. Her father stressed that her screams at night were terrifying.

Colette had two previous sessions in which she experienced severe birth trauma and screamed in rage and terror. After the first session there was a distinct improvement, she could be pacified and touched but was still not sleeping. Before the second session, on talking with the mother, Carmel discovered the mother's sleep pattern when carrying Colette had been one of studying night and day for her external exams. They both agreed that this could have set up Colette's own disturbed sleep patterns.

After the second session in which Colette explored a little more of her birth trauma, the crying ceased and she was able to stay quiet and play with her toys.

She was brought back for a third session into the *Amethyst* training group for review, with her three year old brother Timmy. There had been considerable improvement and she was much better at allowing people to touch her. The members of the group were shown how to develop a session playing with toys, how to help the child get used to strangers, how to play birth games, for example, crawling through daddy's legs to restimulate the birth trauma and desensitise it. The two children got great affirmation from the group.

The major game for the session was the earthquake game where Colette was placed between her parents as they sat closely facing each other on the floor, with their arms around each other. Earthquake music or womb sounds were played and the children made their own sounds.

Colette went her own way in this session. She automatically regressed into her birth process. She made an attempt at being born but retreated. She stayed contentedly in her "womb" and then quietly tried again to be born but again retracted. In her birth she had her head engaged for a long time. In this rebirthing session, when her head started crowning Carmel gently placed her hands on Colette's head, with Timmy helping. Carmel affirmed Colette all the time—"Good girl—do it your way", while her hands were gently massaging Colette's head. At this point Collette's head was engaged, her nose was squashed—so no pressure was applied.

With distressed crying, her head appeared and one little hand popped out. The 'hole' for her to appear from was beneath her parent's locked arms. Colette was eased out gently by Carmel, helped by Timmy, and handed immediately to her mother and father for instant bonding.

The recovery time for Collette was rapid and her parent's made a human boat for the little girl and her brother to sit in while quiet music was played. After this session the parents said that Colette was a new child.

A FINAL WORD—THERE IS SOME HOPE

The group of adults who observed Colette experiencing her birth were very moved by it. One member put it succinctly:

> All I could think of was how privileged Timmy and Colette were. I was looking at Colette and she was so happy and content at being in the womb. She had her mother and father there, as she was coming out, and she could have come out at any time—but there was a residue of her birth. Once she got out there was this cocoon in the womb of family relationships that she could actually go into.

I heard someone retort that it could be horrific putting a baby through this when you see the pain they go through. But the healing is saving them from a lifetime of pain. It may be far better to treat birth related trauma in the early years, through the many techniques that are now available, to prevent dysfunctional behaviour emerging in later years from unresolved traumatisation.

REFERENCES

Chamberlain, D. (1988) *Babies Remember Birth* now republished as (1998) *The Mind of Your Newborn Baby.* North Atlantic Books.

Emerson, W. (1984) Infant and Birth Refacilitation. Two papers. Available from Human Potential Resources, 4940 Bodega Ave., Petaluma, CA 94952, USA.

Emerson, W. (1989) Unpublished Papers.

Foder, N. (1949) *The Search for the Beloved: A clinical investigation of the trauma of birth birth and prenatal conditioning.* New Hyde Park, New York Univ. Books.

Grof, S. (1975) *Realms of the Human Unconscious,* New York: Viking Press.

Janov, A. (1973) *The Feeling Child,* New York: Simon and Schuster.

Lake, F. (1978) Treating Psychosomatic disorders related to Birth Trauma. *Journal of Psychosomatic Research,* 22, 227–238.

Mott, F. (1952) *Play Therapy with Children,* Great Britain: The Integration Press.

Peerbolte, L.M. (1975) *Psychic energy in prenatal dynamics, parapsychology, peak experiences,* Wassenaar: Severe Publishers.

Oaklander, V. (1978) *Windows to our Children: A gestalt therapy approach to children and adolescents,* Real People Press: Moab, Utah.

O'Moore, M. (1994) *Handbook on Bullying,* Trinity College: Dublin.

Verny, T. with John Kelly (1981 & 1986) *The Secret Life of the Unborn Child,* New York: Dell.

Ward, S.A. (1985) "Stressful Pregnancies and Traumatic Births resulting in possible behaviour, emotional and learning difficulties." Unpublished Masters Thesis, Nottingham University, UK.

Journal of Prenatal and Perinatal Psychology and Health, 13(3–4), Spring/Summer 1999

Prenatal and Perinatal Foundations of Moral Development

Millicent Adams Dosh, MA

ABSTRACT: Drawing upon an impressive body of writing and published research in the area of prenatal and perinatal psychology, the author here presents her own thoughts about the critical importance of the prenatal and perinatal period as foundational for the later moral development and behavior of the person. She argues that any design for moral education must take this early period into account. Mutual connection or affectional bonding between people, when honored during the time of prenatal life, birth, breastfeeding and early infancy, acts as a template influencing how later experiences are felt, perceived and integrated. The origins of love as well as of alienation lie in prenatal and perinatal interactions with mother, caretakers and culture.

INTRODUCTION

An individual person's moral development and behavior begin with, and are influenced by, prenatal and perinatal experiences. Any design or model for moral education must acknowledge the formative influence of these prenatal and perinatal experiences on later moral development.

If we want a child to grow into an adult capable of moral behavior that contributes to the good of self and society, early formative experiences that facilitate such behavior are desirable. How do we foster such formation? Nature has evolved a biological design for human development that is dependent on mutual connection and affectional bonding between people. When honored, this biological design leads a person from conception to maturity through death with a sense of belonging to a group. A person cannot become fully human, capable of functioning in a group, without this sense of belonging. Within the group, the individual can be guided toward moral conduct.

Millicent Adams Dosh, MA is a Montessori educator and post-partum doula. This Article was presented at the First Conference on the Ethics of Parenting held by the Center for Applied Ethics, Pace University, New York City, February 1999. Correspondence may be directed to email: doshx001@tc.umn.edu or 4124 Harriet Avenue South Minneapolis, Minnesota 55409 (Phone) 612-827-1818.

PREGNANCY, BIRTH AND BREASTFEEDING

The bonding experiences of prenatal life, birth, breastfeeding and early infancy are particularly formative, and act as a tincture or template influencing how later experiences are felt, perceived, and integrated. These essential aspects of prenatal and perinatal life promote affectional bonding and mutual connection, and form the development of trust and confidence in the new, sentient being. This requires a welcomed pregnancy and a healthy prenatal life, because the mother-child bond begins here.

Pregnancy

The baby in utero shares space with its mother and thus is affected by every aspect of her life and her wider world. The attitude of the mother toward her pregnancy is a major aspect of the womb environment absorbed by the baby. If the mother welcomes the conception and is happy, her body chemistry benefits the baby. If the mother is tentative, fearful, rejecting, or hostile to her new condition, the baby's health will be compromised to some degree. A pregnant mother and baby are physically and emotionally connected. This symbiotic relationship will continue for a time outside the womb until the child differentiates self from mother (Mahler, 1975), but the emotional connections begin here.

Womb experiences are integral to an individual's history. If, for example, a baby becomes accustomed to a womb world shared with a twin, life has peer companionship from the beginning with both the comfort of a playmate and the stress of crowding. If one twin dies, which happens frequently, there is early loss and grieving. If the surviving twin hears the story of the loss from earliest days, the words of narrative can be matched and integrated with his or her memory of the felt experience. The reality of loss will always be a part of this child's life story, but need not be overwhelming by being left unnamed. What has power, and is later acted out by an individual, is experience which has not been brought to awareness and integrated. Language and storytelling help a child integrate experience.

Many women experience initial ambivalence at the confirmation of a pregnancy if it has been unplanned, but there seems to be strong evidence that an unwanted pregnancy can affect the child. In *The Mind of your Newborn Baby* (Chamberlain, 1998), David Chamberlain summarizes a study of 8,000 privileged married women who received early prenatal care under a comprehensive health care program. They were divided into two groups, those whose pregnancies were wanted or unwanted. The babies of unwanted pregnancies had two and a half times the risk of death in the first twenty-eight days of life compared with the babies from wanted pregnancies. This study was done by Bustan and Coker (1994).

With the advent of the use of ultrasound, it has been possible to observe babies' reactions to changes in the womb environment. Practitioners have noted that babies stop swallowing for a time following their mothers' use of alcohol, show distress following use of cocaine and stop fetal breathing within the hour following the mother's cigarette smoking. If mom is a chronic alcoholic, the baby may need to ingest the alcohol for the duration of the pregnancy for survival, but could be born with fetal alcohol syndrome. Or, the baby might initiate premature leave taking of an unhealthy environment, either before or after viability outside the womb is possible. Premature birth could lead to other life complications and challenges. Premature infants experience many needs that should be met with tenderness and compassion. Mothers at times need help in overcoming feelings of disappointment and guilt in giving birth to a premature baby, even when there has not been any chemical abuse during the pregnancy. If unsupported, such mothers can remain less emotionally available to their infants who need their comfort and care to thrive and grow strong and confident (Madsen,1994). With support and care, such mothers can establish a warm relationship with their fragile infants even in the face of adversity. Thus, the prenatal experience of the baby has meaning and sometimes lifelong implications.

If a mother suffers abuse during the pregnancy, the event is part of the baby's neural record. The baby feels the shock and associated feelings. One of the most severe traumas that a prenate can experience is an attempted and failed abortion. Adults who embody this history wrestle with profound distress and need support and therapy to avoid self destructive behavior and make a commitment to live. Prenatal interaction with the mother is not merely passive. The baby in utero enjoys direct conversation and will respond with kicks and movement. Beatriz Manrique, a Venezuelan psychologist, conducted an extensive research study on prenatal bonding. In her study mothers and fathers were involved in talking to their babies in the womb. The six-year follow up study showed that the children fared better in almost every way from the attention given to them while in the womb. One of the unexpected outcomes of the project was that the participating fathers, who for the most part were unmarried and were expected to abandon the mothers, tended to remain with the mothers and assume responsibility for parenting their children (Manrique, 1995). Babies will recognize their parents' voices after birth and prefer them to strangers (Verny & Kelly, 1981). Their relationship with their parents is nine months old by the time of birth.

Birth

As recent studies show, the primary role in initiating the birth process belongs to the child. An ecological birth promotes bonding because it respects and supports the child's agency in initiating labor and engaging in a stressful but safe passage into a new and welcoming environment.

Birth is the first major transition of the human person, from the environmental matrix of the womb to a new matrix in the arms of the mother, at her breast, in the context the mother's world. The baby's associations with this first transition experience might be that transitions are long and painful, short and intense, ending in a warm welcome or ending with a permanent separation from the birth mother, drug free or under the influence of narcotics, alert or sedated. These aspects of birth may become aspects of all future life transitions, replicated in various ways with subsequent transitional events. The point I want to make is that they are not neutral and without consequence. They are encoded in the baby's neural memory bank.

On the physiological level, interactions in the perinatal period influence healthy functioning of the immune system, hormone production, and neuro-cardiac patterns in the baby (Prescott, 1996). Interactions are key to the baby's emotional life. For example, in our technological birth settings, it is often very difficult for a birthing mother to enter into that part of herself which knows how to collaborate with her child as s/he exits the womb. The task requires concentration and sometimes solitude (Odent, 1992). The hospital setting, well set up for every emergency, can sometimes work against this process.

Frequently replicated studies have shown that if a mother receives continuous emotional support during labor and delivery, her labor will tend to be shorter, that medical interventions, including drugs, will be fewer, and the probability of a C-section will be lower (Klaus & Klaus, 1993). Such benefits are enjoyed by the baby whose efforts require a lower output of stress hormones and produce quicker results. The newborn is better able to put into practice his or her innate skills.

Immediately following birth, if the mother holds her infant skin to skin, heart to heart, there is a rapid decrease in the baby's stress hormone levels. Conversely, if the baby is separated from the mother, high stress hormone levels may remain for as long as six months (Pearce, 1977). If drug free and alert, the newborn is able to crawl to the breast and begin both suckling and face to face communication as it gazes at its mother (Klaus & Klaus, 1998). If allowed to root and suckle at the breast, the baby will experience the pleasant effects of seratonin and oxytocin. The pleasure of belonging is thus strengthened. Competent interactive patterns in the sentient neonate are central to the emergence of an adult capable of altruism, civic responsibility and service, and these patterns can be engaged immediately. Aristotle wrote that we are what we repeatedly do. A baby's repeated success at securing his own life necessities reinforces the sense of competent functioning within human relationships. Every experience matters, and becomes encoded in the matter and functioning of the baby's body.

Breastfeeding

Breastfeeding is biologically designed to aid the baby in developing an affectional bond with the mother. If this bond is strong and secure, the baby will use it as a secure base from which to move out and develop other social interactions. Breastfeeding infants, by discovering and practicing successful strategies in obtaining nourishment, develop powerful neurological, immunological and endocrinology patterns that give them competence in satisfying physical and emotional needs. Breastfeeding infants tend to have fewer upper respiratory infections and so enjoy better health in general (Newman, 1995). When the baby suckles, nerve endings in both baby's mouth and mother's nipple are stimulated. These impulses send signals to the spinal chords and then to the hypothalamus in the brains of both mother and baby, where oxytocin is released and drips to the pituitary gland, moving into the bloodstream of both mother and baby. The oxytocin causes a letdown of milk in the mother, and causes contractions and clamping of the uterus which protects the new mother against hemorrhaging. The baby, then, both manufactures oxytocin and ingests it from the mother's milk. The brain also releases endorphins, the body's natural opiates, which contribute to the pleasurable experience of both mother and baby. Both experience euphoria and slight sleepiness and their pain threshold rises. This process helps the mother and baby to fall in love with one another (Uvnäs-Moberg, 1989). Thus breastfeeding assists the baby in becoming pleasure tolerant and capable of engaging in intimate human love relationships with ease. If these and other aspects of prenatal and perinatal interaction are respected, positive

consequences for the healthy moral development of the individual follow.

INTERACTION OF INFANTS WITH ADULT CARETAKERS

Adult caretakers of babies are vital resources for infants who are
developing foundations for lifelong patterns of interaction with others
and society as a whole. A neonate's earliest interactions with mother,
caretakers, and community have an impact on later biological, intellectual, intrapersonal, interpersonal, and social development. This is
precisely because these interactions occur so early in the baby's life,
during the time when the brain/nervous system, being in such a rapid
state of growth, is creating links which influence future pathways and
patterns in the neurological, immune and endocrine systems. The
work of Candace Pert, a neuro scientist, shows that we no longer can
pretend that there is no molecular connection between emotions and
body chemistry. The molecules of emotion (peptides, proteins and re-
ceptors) are measurable and site specific (Pert, 1997). The baby manufactures an array of peptides, and what is desirable is that the adults
responsible for a baby provide optimal conditions for the production
of pleasure hormones. We want our babies to be pleasure prone. We
want happy babies in order to most easily bring forth happy adults.

The child, from the beginning of life, is his own agent within the
context of his relationship with mother in finding a source for food.
After birth, a newborn is capable of creeping all the way from the
mother's feet to the breast and finding the breast to suckle. Marshall
and Phyllis Klaus have discovered in their observations that the baby
even licks his hands and marks the breast, claiming it with his own
saliva (Klaus & Klaus, 1998). When hungry, the baby signals, first
through body language and later by crying, to alert the mother of his
need. If a baby is consistently ignored when hungry and is fed only at
the rigid determination of the caretaker and on her schedule, the baby
may give up a sense of his own agency in procuring food.

Very early child rearing practices such as feeding discipline or sleeping discipline either acknowledge this agency of the child or determine
that the child's agency is to be crushed and made to conform to a norm
established by the parent. No matter what system is established, its
impact on later moral development is certain.

There are fundamentalist child rearing practices that use this
knowledge to break the child's "will" as they put it, and socialize the
child into compliance, preparing the child for absolute obedience to an

external lawmaker, and not to their own inner guide. This world view is in sharp contrast to one that requires the vital functioning of adults able to use their own voices in a participatory society, dependent on dialogue and consensus decision-making. Each time a child signals to a caretaker that it is hungry and the caretaker responds with affirmation and feeding, the child's agency is strengthened. If kept alive and affirmed, the child's sense of power and agency will mature. Children will learn to recognize others' needs as legitimate because their own are validated. They will learn cooperation and mutual respect and help to build a society where individual needs are met in the context of the common good.

Using Transaction Analysis language and models, there is a Primary Obligatory Symbiosis (Phillips, 1975) at the beginning of life when a baby, with only the Child Ego State, must "borrow" both Parent Ego State and Adult Ego State from a parent (Stewart & Joines, 1987). If the parent is mature, and not using the baby to meet her own primary needs, the baby can develop within this necessary symbiotic relationship and move gradually toward the individuation process. Conversely, the child's development can become skewed at an early age if it becomes the parent's caretaker. These early interpersonal dynamics, once formed, influence later moral activity of the individual. For example, a child may abandon a healthy pattern of signaling her own needs, deferring to the emotional needs of an immature parent, thus diminishing the child's perception of her own needs and setting the stage for codependency and addiction patterns later in life.

All members of a family are called on to make adjustments when a newborn or adopted child enters the scene. Adults and children must invent functional communication, all working toward the common good of the whole family. The baby is an active participant in this realignment process. Skills developed in the family are then brought by the child to an ever-widening number of communities and put into practice as his or her world expands. The child grows in physical, emotional, intellectual and social tolerance of new and challenging situations. The parents, through language and modeling, mediate the child's extended experience with neighborhood, extended family, school, and so on. There needs to be a safe place to which the child can return when overwhelmed or when in need of sharing and celebration of new growth. Healthy grounding for meeting these later challenging situations in life are best established in the earliest relationships of infancy.

CONCLUSION

We want a child's brain/neurological system, endocrine system and immune system to gradually develop both a tolerance of and pleasurable enjoyment of interaction with other people. We want this interaction to serve the child's personal development and his or her sense of membership in the family and social group. Thus equipped with an embodied self-confidence, the child will meet self-needs, demonstrate empathy for others, participate as a functional member of society and, with personal power intact, be of service in a democratic society.

Adequate attention to this critical prenatal and perinatal period is not a guarantee against future deviation. Trauma can happen at any time, and it can be so severe as to shatter the trust of a person and cause subsequent behavior to be skewed and damaging to the individual and/or society. Such a trauma appears to have happened to Theodore Kaczyinski, the Unabomber. At the age of nine months, he was hospitalized for a drug reaction. For one week he was tied to his bed and was touched by no one. His mother reported that when he came home he was listless and never the same again ("Kaczynski's mental state," 1997). Life is fragile, and a baby's life can be abruptly disrupted by death of a primary caretaker, by adoption, by illness, or by abuse. But a gentle and loving beginning can provide the baby with a basic orientation, a focal point, a reference point on which to base future strategies to further his or her own development and to heal from life's adversities.

Religious institutions, which act as important moral guidance centers in our society for many, and which often develop highly sophisticated codes of moral conduct, must acknowledge this early period as significant, and must weigh its importance in their deliberations and teachings. Personnel who run daycare centers, preschools, elementary and secondary schools as well as colleges and universities need to acknowledge prenatal and perinatal influences so as to demonstrate compassion toward young children and students who are grappling with prenatal and perinatal trauma and pain for which they have not yet been offered any healing process. Institutions must consider the validity of including information about an individual's earliest period of life as an important portion of their whole story. When we teach ethics, we must include substantive information about these influential months of life.

Where the child's agency is crushed and coerced by authoritarian rule, there is a loss to society of the energy and contribution that the individual might have made. At worst, there may develop a character with suppressed and unconscious rage that later is inflicted on society itself by murder, rape, or overpowering political rule. We have such examples in Adolf Hitler, severely abused in childhood, and in Sadham Hussein, an abortion attempt survivor. If the biological design for development is thwarted, and a person fails to seek and receive what is necessary in order to trust and enjoy mutual connection to a human group, the individual may eventually inflict harm on self or society. A child without feelings is a child without a conscience (Magid & Mc-Kelvey, 1987).

We need to view moral development on a continuum, from conception through death. Since the origins of love as well as of alienation and violence lie in prenatal and perinatal life, everything possible must be done on behalf of the prenate and neonate to ensure that he or she grows into a healthy, feeling child. Any comprehensive design for moral education must recognize the critical importance of this early foundation.

REFERENCES

Bustan, M. N. & Coker, A. L. (1994). Maternal attitude toward pregnancy and the risk of neonatal death. *American Journal of Public Health,* 84(3), 411–414.

Chamberlain, D. (1998). *The mind of your newborn baby.* Berkeley: North Atlantic Books.

Kaczynski's mental state is focus as the Unabomber trial begins. (1997, November 12). *Star Tribune,* p. 6a.

Klaus, M. H., Kennell, J. H. & Klaus, P. H. (1995). *Bonding: Building the foundations of secure attachment and independence.* Reading, MA: Addison-Wesley.

Klaus, M. H. & Klaus, P. H. (1993). *Mothering the mother.* Reading, MA: Addison-Wesley.

Klaus, M. H. & Klaus, P. H. (1998). *Your amazing newborn.* Reading, MA: Perseus Books.

Madsen, L. (1994). *Rebounding from childbirth: Toward emotional recovery.* Westport, CT: Bergin & Garvey.

Magid, K. & McKelvey, C. A. (1987). *High risk: Children without a conscience.* Toronto: Bantam.

Mahler, M., Pine, F. & Bergman, A. (1975). *The psychological birth of the human infant: Symbiosis and individuation.* New York: Basic Books.

Manrique, B. (1995). Love effaces violence: panel on breaking the cycle of violence. *Pre- and Perinatal Psychology Journal,* 10(2), 83–87.

Newman, J. (1995, December). How breast milk protects newborns: some of the molecules and cells in human milk actively help infants stave off infection. *Scientific American,* pp. 76–79.

Odent, M. (1992). *The nature of birth and breastfeeding.* Westport, CT: Bergin & Garvey.

Pearce, J. C. (1977). *Magical child: Rediscovering nature's plan for our children.* New York: E. P. Dutton.

Pert, C. (1997). *Molecules of emotion: Why you feel the way you feel.* New York: Scribner.

Phillips, R. D. (1975). *Structural symbiotic systems: Correlations with ego states, behavior and physiology.* Unpublished manuscript, Chapel Hill, NC.

Prescott, J. W. (1996). The origins of human love and violence. *Pre- and Perinatal Psychology Journal,* 10(3), 143–188.
Stewart, I. & Joines, V. (1987). *T. A. today: A new introduction to transactional analysis.* Nottingham and Chapel Hill: Lifespace Publishing.
Uvnäs-Moberg, K. (1989, July). The gastrointestinal tract in growth and reproduction. *Scientific American,* pp. 78–83.
Verny, T. R. & Kelly, J. (1981). *The secret life of the unborn child.* New York: Dell.

Journal of Prenatal and Perinatal Psychology and Health, 13(3–4), Spring/Summer 1999

The Biopsychosocial Transactional Model of Development: The Beginning of The Formation of An Emergent Sense of Self in the Newborn

Donis Eichhorn, RN, Ph.D. and Thomas R. Verny, MD, D Psych, FRCP(C)

ABSTRACT: The rationale for providing an emotionally positive experience for both the infant's beginning "emergent sense of self" (Stern, 1985) and for his return to the "Secure Base" (Bowlby, 1988) of his mother vis-a-vis his innate ability for "self attachment" within the first hour after birth (Righard & Alade, 1990) is explored.Giving birth and being born are both physiological and psychological processes. Since it is now known (Schore, 1994; Shore, 1997) that the interaction between the infant and his mother creates the structure and organization of the infant's developing brain, it is important to become aware of and responsive to the self attachment research regarding the *Amazing Newborn* (Righard & Alade, 1990; Klaus & Klaus, 1998).

INTRODUCTION

Knowledge about infant mental health and development has grown extensively in the last two decades. Through systematic observation, research and clinical intervention, there is now a more detailed and sophisticated understanding of the factors that contribute to either adaptive or maladaptive patterns of development. This knowledge, in turn, has led to an increasing awareness of the importance of prevention and intervention in creating (or restoring) favorable conditions for the infant's development and mental health (Zero to Three/National Center for Clinical Infant Programs, 1994).

Donis Eichhorn, RN, Ph.D. is Associate Clinical Professor, Dept. of Pediatrics & Center for Child & Familiy Studies, the University of California, Davis. She may be reached at 1509 Del Dayo Drive, Carmichael, Ca 95608. Phone (916) 752-2888. Thomas R. Verny, MD, D Psych, FRCP(C) is the founder of APPPAH. He is considered one of the world's leading authorities on pre- and perinatal psychology. This paper is the result of research, under his direction, during the course of study in pre- and perinatal psychology he pioneered in conjunction with the Department of Human Development, Prenatal and Perinatal Psychology Program, St. Mary's University, Minneapolis. He may be contacted at 36 Madison Ave., Toronto, Ontario M5R251, Canada.

THE RELATIONSHIP BETWEEN SECURE ATTACHMENT AND THE PROTECTION OF BIOLOGICAL FUNCTION

The development of new research tools, such as brain imaging technologies, have led neuroscientists to realize that the infant's development not only takes place within the context of the caregiving relationship (Siegel, 1998), but also that the quality of the developmental process of the brain—*beginning even before birth* is affected by environmental conditions, including the kind of nourishment, care, surroundings and appropriate stimulation the prenate and the infant receive from caregivers. It has also become more clear that human development and learning depend critically on the interplay between nature (an individual's genetic endowment) and nurture (the quality of the infant-parent relationship). Responsive caregiving not only meets the baby's basic needs for nourishment and warmth, but also takes into account rhythms, preferences and moods. The brain is a mirror reflection of the organization of the patterning, timing, nature, frequency and quality of both the interactional and relational experiences of the young child (Perry, Pollard, Blakeley, Baker & Vigilante, 1995).

The qualities of both responsive caregiving and the ways in which the caregiver mediates the infant's contact with his environment not only affects the developmental process, but even more importantly, directly affects the formation of neural pathways and patterns of neuronal connectivity within the brain (Shore, 1997). The neural systems underlying emotional, behavioral, cognitive, social and physiological functioning depend upon the inherent capacity of the brain to organize and give meaning to the experiences of infancy and childhood (Bleiberg, 1995). By age three, the brain is 90 percent the size of the adult brain and the majority of the key neural systems have been organized (Thoenen, 1995). As Eisenberg (1995) succinctly wrote, "the human brain is constructed socially."

It now appears that the need for a strong, secure attachment to a nurturing caregiver (Ainsworth, Blehar, Waters & Wall, 1976; Bowlby, 1988) not only promotes healthy development, but also seems to have the protective biological function of "immunizing" an infant to some degree against the adverse effects of later stress or trauma (Gunnar, 1996 in Shore, 1997). Megan R. Gunnar of the University of Minnesota has gauged children's reaction to stress by measuring the levels of a steroid hormone called cortisol in their saliva. Traumatic events, whether physical or psychological, can elevate an individual's cortisol level. In turn, cortisol affects metabolism, the immune system, and the brain. Cortisol alters the brain by making it vulnerable to processes that destroy neurons and reduce the number of synapses in certain parts of the brain. Children who have chronically high levels of cortisol have been shown to experience more developmental delays—cognitive, motor, and social—than other children (Gunnar, 1996).

By six months prenatally, the nerve cells are in place in the brain. However, at birth, the brain is remarkably unfinished. The number of connections (synapses) from cell to cell depend on experience. The baby's experience (perception) of the quality of both the interactional process and the infant-caregiver relationship creates the connections between the cells and the infant's ability to process information. The fact that the brain matures in the world, rather than in the womb, means that young children are deeply affected by their early experiences and interactions which determine brain structure, thus shaping the way people learn, think, and behave for the rest of their lives (Reiner Foundation, 1997).

THE ACTIVE ROLE OF THE BABY ON BIRTH

The outside world of the infant is experienced through the senses—seeing, hearing, smelling, touching, and tasting—enabling the brain to create or modify connections (Reiner Foundation, 1997). Bonnie Bainbridge Cohen's work of "Body-Mind Centering" has explored developmental patterns and anatomical systems. She has identified the mind states and movement quality associated with the activities of specific patterns and systems both in the prenate and during the first year of life. Cohen (1993) states that this period of development "is when the relationship of the perceptual process (the way one sees) and the motor process (the way one moves or acts in the the world) is established". Cohen has also expanded the list of the five major senses to include the sensations of movement and visceral activity. Cohen believes that "all mind patternings are expressed in movement, through the body. And, that all physically moving patterns have a mind" (Cohen, 1993). To understand the active role of the baby in birthing one must enter the kinesthetic realm of the prenate (Cohen, 1993; Burns, 1998).

Recent discoveries in the development and neurobiology of memory have given insights into the nature of how our minds respond to experience which influences later functioning (Milner, Kandel & Squire, 1998 in Siegel, 1998). Two major forms of memory have been described—implicit and explicit. For the purpose of this paper, only implicit memory will be discussed. Implicit memory includes a range of processes such as emotional, behavioral, perceptual and possibly somatosensory memory (Siegel, 1998). These forms are present at birth and are thought to be carried out in areas of the brain that include their functions such as the amygdala and other areas of the limbic system (emotional memory), basal ganglia and motor cortex (behavioral memory), and the sensory cortex (perceptual memory). These regions are relatively well developed at birth and capable of responding to experience by alterations in the synaptic connections within their circuitry, the essence of "memory encoding". Another aspect of implicit memory is the ability of the mind to form schema or mental models of experience. Such mental models are a fundamental part of how attachment experiences are formed and influence the child's later relationships (Bowlby, 1969; Siegel, 1998.)

RECENT RESEARCH REGARDING THE *AMAZING NEWBORN*

The fairly recent discovery of the newborn's ability to crawl up to the mother's breast, attach himself unassisted and to suckle *correctly* (Righard & Alade, 1990) was published in The Lancet, 1990, 336: 1105–07. Righard and Alade looked at two groups of newborn babies. In the first group, the infant was placed on the mother's abdomen and within 50 minutes most infants had self-attached to the breast and were suckling correctly. In the second group the newborn babies were removed from the mother's abdomen, bathed, measured and replaced on the abdomen. The infants in this group, from an unmedicated birth, self-attached but half of them had a faulty suckling pattern. Most of the infants from a medicated birth were too drowsy to be able to suckle at all. Righard and Alade's research has been extensively elaborated by Marshall Klaus, M.D. and Phyllis Klaus, C.S.W., M.F.C.C. in their recent (1998) exquisitely prepared book *Your Amazing Newborn*. Raymond Castellino, D.C., R.P.P. with Debby Takikawa, D.C. and Samantha Wood, M.A. has also elaborated upon Dr. Righard's research. Dr. Castellino's paper entitled "The Caregiver's Role in Birth and Newborn Self-attachment Needs," was presented at the 8th International Congress of The Association for Pre- and Perinatal Psychology and Health (APPPAH) on "Birth, Love and Relationships" in December of 1997. Castellino, et al., believe that "understanding the delivery self attachment behaviors broadens the perspective of the bonding/ attachment process. That healthy bonding and attachment are the outcome of a whole sequence of events that are somatic, neurophysiological and psychological in nature". In addition Castellino, et al., believe that "babies and mothers who are supported to complete the delivery self attachment sequence immediately after birth will bond more completely, initiate nursing more effectively and be more cooperative with each other as the baby grows".

They also suggest that "the completion of the delivery self attachment sequence at birth will have long lasting positive effects on the baby's neurological, somatic, and psychological development". The Castellino group also point out that the newborn self attachment behaviors are unknowingly and routinely interrupted by hospital obstetric and midwifery practices. Therefore, the possibility of long lasting negative effects may or may not be recognized or even connected to the self attachment experience.

The Need to Integrate Current Infant Mental Health Concepts and Developmental Neurobiological Findings into Caregiving

Utilizing the research concerning:

(1) infant development and mental health
(2) the awareness that the baby has an active role in the birthing process
(3) the recent advances in understanding how the quality of both the caregiving relationship and the infant-parent interactional process affects the structure, organization, and neurochemical architecture of the brain (Schore, 1994).

the following discussion will endeavor:

(1) to make more explicit the concept of infant mental health as defined by Alicia Lieberman, 1998
(2) to investigate the significance of the management of anxiety not only for the developmental process of the infant, but also for the integrity of the formative phases of the "self" (Horner, 1984; Stern, 1985)
(3) to broaden Stern's (1985) concept of the formative phase of the "emergent sense of self" to the *beginning* of the emergent sense of self outside of the womb as manifested in the self attachment experience
(4) to discuss how the interruption of the self attachment process could be experienced as trauma by both the mother and her newborn, and

(5) to urge the need for preventive intervention.

An Infant Mental Health Perspective

In writing about an "Infant Mental Health Perspective" Alicia Lieberman (1998) has identified five main principles that define this point of view:

1. Babies are by nature social creatures
2. Individual differences are an integral component of babies' functioning
3. Every individual exists in a particular social, relational and environmental context that deeply affects the person's functioning
4. Infant mental health practitioners make an effort to understand how behaviors feel from the inside, not just how they look from the outside
5. The intervenor's own feelings and behaviors have a major impact on the intervention.

The first four principles have to do with looking at external behavior as an inner, subjective experience. As mentioned before, babies develop within the context of relationships. The emotional bonds that are formed between the baby and his emotionally significant caregiver build the earliest foundations for mental health by helping the baby feel loved, valued, and competent, as opposed to feeling unwanted, burdensome, and ineffective. It is the passionate "only you" sustaining power of intimate relationships that is at the core of the baby's capacity "to love well and to grow well" (Lieberman, 1998).

The Neuropsychodiological Significance of Self Attachment

Surely, the baby's ability to self-attach gives both the mother and her infant the subjective experience of physical contact and social/emotional intimacy at the earliest kinesthetic, preverbal and neurochemical process of "falling in love" with one another. Since the brain is designed to be social and the limbic system is especially concerned with attachment, emotion and motivation (Shore, 1997), one could assume that the first "schema-of-being-with-another-in-a-certain-way" (Stern, 1995) is being formed that makes biological sense to the biologically "programmed" infant for secure attachment (Bleiberg, 1995). The limbic system, "comprised of cortical and subcortical structures actively selects, organizes and integrates pieces of information into the developing intrapsychic structure of the brain when reality matches the model in the mind", (Settlage, Bemesderfer, Rosenthal, Afterman, & Spielman, 1991; Bleiberg, 1995). A positive self attachment experience is certainly the antithesis of the experiences of the infant who is traumatized during the birthing process, separated from his mother and who is subjected to various uncomfortable procedures. Research indicates that infants do cope in various ways, depending on the continuity and degree of trauma, by adapting, becoming hyper aroused for "fight" or "flight", compartmentalizing or dissociating the experience of unbearable psychic pain from conscious awareness (Bleiberg, 1995; Perry, 1995; Fonagy, 1999).

The baby's active participation in his birthing process (Cohen, 1993) and his self attachment experience (Righard & Adale, 1990); Castellino, et al. (1997) and Klaus & Klaus (1998) can give the baby the experience of:

(1) initiating an internal process on his own (Hoffman, et al., 1998)
(2) experiencing mastery and competence of his abilities (Grey, 1992) during the self attachment process, and
(3) relieving whatever tension and anxiety the baby may have experienced during his birth journey.

Consequently, the baby will feel relaxed, secure and at peace with himself (as evidenced by his affect and his behavior) and with his "emotionally significant other" who is "delighted" and proud of her newborn's accomplishment (Klaus & Klaus, 1998). This precious vignette i.e., the experience of both mother and baby is a lovely example of:

(1) object relations theory (Moberly, 1985)
(2) the beginning of the infant is capacity to experience, endure and regulate affect within a self structure, and
(3) the beginning formation of an internal working model (Bowlby, 1969).

The baby is essentially returning to what hopefully is to become his 'Secure Base' (Bowlby, 1988), back to the smell, the heartbeat, the warmth, and the rhythms of his interuterine experience with his mother. This self attachment process is also a good description of the beginning of Mahler's Separation-Individuation process as described in the book, *The Psychological Birth of the Human Infant* (Mahler, Pine & Bergman, 1975).

The Beginning of an Emergent Sense of Self

Being in tune with and empathic about the impact of the baby's birthing experience and being aware of his needs during the journey from inside the mother into the world which creates the need to re-connect with the mother is another core concept in infant mental health (emotional refueling from an emotionally available mother) (Mahler, et al., 1975; Akhtar, Kramer & Parens, 1996; Robinson, Emde, Korfmacher, 1997). Allowing and facilitating the newborn's ability to self-attach also enhances the developmental process of mu-tual emotional regulation between mother and infant which underlies the quality of the attachment process (Tronick, 1989).

In order for the infant to develop the capacity for self-regulation, he has to experience the ministrations of a "self-regulating other" who soothes, comforts and contains the infant's tension, anxiety and dis-tress (Horner, 1982; Winnicott, 1987; Akhtar, Kramer & Parens, 1996). Surely there is physiological and emotional relaxation in the relationship, when the newborn is able to complete his birthing pro-cess, his need to self attach, and to suckle, as Dr. Righard described, *correctly*.

The Relationship Between Key Experiences and Trauma

As mentioned previously, it is now known that the continuity of early experiences of trauma or abuse, whether in utero or after birth can interfere with the development of the subcortical and limbic areas of the brain, resulting in extreme anxiety, depression, and/or the in-ability to form healthy attachments to others (Shore, 1997). Therefore, it is important to minimize the possibility of experiential trauma. Re-searchers have now generally agreed that both the quality of caregiv-ing and the security of attachment affect children's later capacity for empathy, emotional regulation, and behavioral control. Bruce Perry of Baylor University (in Shore, 1997) asserts that when *key experiences* are minimal or absent, the result may be an inability to modulate impulsivity, immature emotional and behavioral functioning, and (in combination with other developmental experiences) a predisposition to violence (Shore, 1997). Kennell and Klaus (1998), pioneers in re-searching parent-infant bonding since the 1970's, continue to reiterate that encouraging mother-infant contact from birth on and rooming-in could increase breastfeeding significantly and decrease the incidence of failure to thrive, abuse, neglect, and abandonment of infants.

There can be little debate with Castellino, et al. (1997), Kennell and

Klaus, 1998, and Klaus and Klaus, 1998 that the newborn's need to complete his birthing process and to initiate a successful breast feeding experience is most significant and is, in keeping with Bruce Perry's view, a "key experience" for both the mother and her newborn. The same researchers also deplore the common practice in the contemporary hospital birth which interrupts the self attachment process and interferes with the baby's transitional quest reconnect to his mother after birth.

It would seem that the initial anxiety experienced by the infant upon his physiological separation from the mother is "traumatic anxiety" as defined by Horner (1984). Any experience that overwhelms the infant's emergent sense of self during the first three months causes psychic trauma (Horner, 1984), which not only interferes with the infant-parent relationship per se, and the initiation of a successful breast feeding experience (Righard & Alade, 1990; Castellino, et al., 1997; Kennell & Klaus, 1998; Klaus & Klaus, 1998), but also interferes with the development of the subcortical and limbic portion of the brain in terms of neurological connections and neural circuitry (Siegel, 1998).

The meaning of traumatic anxiety according to Schecter, (1980 in Horner, 1984) is that the infant misses someone who is loved and emphasizes the importance of the relationship per se. Horner, however, considers the significance of the relationship in terms of its developmental function of forming intrapsychic structure. Schecter does concur with Horner that "traumatic anxiety" occurs whenever the formative process of the self is overwhelmed or disorganized. With the advent of recent brain research, it does seem that there is a built-in psychobiological response to distress or trauma when reality does not match the model in the mind (Bleiberg, 1995). Since the newborn has the capacity to self attach fairly soon after birth, one can only assume that "this is the way it is supposed to be."

The three to four year journey toward object constancy is a developmental process of slowly acquiring intrapsychic structure and psychic representations of the mother/caregiver, who has the capacity to modify the baby's emotional, physical or psychological pain (McDougall, 1989; Settlage, et al., 1991; Bemporad, 1995; Akhtar, et al., 1996; Fonagy, 1999). The obstetrical staff in the delivery room essentially become the "mother" to the mother (since caregiving is a parallel process). When the mother is incapable of shielding her infant from traumatic overstimulation and cannot prevent negative experiences (being weighed, measured, drops put into the eyes and heel sticks), the baby seems to become overwhelmed, confused, fragmented, and disorganized (as evidenced by his affect and behavior) and could experience the dissolution of any sense of self that may be in the formative stage. This dissolution, in itself, is terrifying and emotionally painful for the infant (Horner, 1982). In addition, the steroid hormone cortisol level is probably rising in response to the trauma (Gunnar, 1996) (a future area for research). Conversely, the mother feels "abandoned and helpless" (Castellino, 1997). The obstetrical team is in charge and the quality of the experience has been diminished and compromised.

Since the infant's preverbal language is affect and behavior (Brazelton & Cramer, 1990) his "traumatic anxiety" is expressed by crying when separated from his mother as noted by Righard & Adale (1990), Castellino et al. (1997), and Klaus & Klaus (1998) as well as by psychic disorganization, and as a result the infant is not able to nurse effectively when finally put to the breast (Righard & Adale, 1990; Kennell & Klaus, 1998). This experience has also been imprinted at the somatic level of the newborn (Castellino, 1997; Siegel, 1998). The implicit memory of this experience can be evoked and expressed when the infant is confronted with a similar experience. The infant's future affective and behavioral expression of emotional/psychic pain and/or disorganization may be a puzzle to his caregivers. Perhaps, by not connecting the infant's subsequent behavior with the missing process of the self attachment experience and thus having difficulty with breast feeding, the mother may give up in frustration and puzzlement and decide to bottle feed instead. Fortunately, Castellino, Cohen and others are studying this process and are beginning to understand how to resolve some of the trauma that occurs during and after the birthing process.

CONCLUSION: THE NEED FOR PREVENTIVE INTERVENTION

The process of giving birth (for the mother) and the process of being born (for the infant) is both a physiological and a psychological process. The possibility of providing an emotionally significant experience for the beginning of a secure attachment relationship between the infant and his mother does exist. The principles of both the Mother-Friendly Childbirth Initiative (Coalition for Improving Maternity Services, 1996) and the Baby Friendly Initiative (Kovach, 1996) are designed to support consumers who want birth centers and hospitals to be more mother, baby and father friendly. Since development takes place within the context of a relationship, perhaps creating a "Relationship Friendly Initiative" could make an implicit process more explicit (Siegel, 1996, 1998).

There is need for preventive intervention. The question of how to translate research findings and theoretical concepts into clinical practice provides both the opportunity and the danger. How these findings are presented to enhance growth and decrease resistance and defensiveness on the part of the health care team is now the challenge which needs to be explored in various settings, i.e., health care delivery systems, professional curriculum, preparation for childbirth and parenting classes, hospital and birth center staffs, and the general public. As so aptly put by one of the participants in one of the Continuing Education Seminars for The Program for Infant/Toddler Caregivers, "when there is enough collective consciousness" about the significance of the competence of the newborn, the quality of caregiving relationships and the relationship between infant-parent interaction and brain development, then the possibility of change may occur.

REFERENCES

Ainsworth, M.D.S., Blehar, M.D., Waters, E., & Wall, S. (1978). *Patterns of Attachment: A Psychological Study of the Strange Situation*. New Jersey: Erlbaum.

Akhtar, S., Kramer, S., & Parens, H. (1996). *The Internal Mother*. New Jersey: Jason Aronson Inc.

Bemporad, S. (1995). *Babies can't wait*. The Signal, Newsletter of the World Association for Infant Mental Health. 3 (3) page 1.

Bleiberg, E. (1995). *Transgenerational Transmission of Attachment Pattern*. Audio Tape from Menninger Continuing Education #030395E 1-800-288-7377.

Bowlby, J. (1988). *A Secure Base*. New York: Basic Books.

Brazelton, T.B. & Cramer, B. (1990). *The Earliest Relationship: Parents, Infants, and the Drama of Early Attachment*. Reading, Massachusetts: Addison-Wesley Publishing Company.

Burns, C. (1998). *The Active Role of the Baby in Birthing*. (unpublished paper) 2228 Seabury Avenue, Minneapolis, MN 55406. 612/339-4097.

Castellino, R. with Takikawa, D. & Wood, S. (1997). *The Caregiver Is Role in Birth and Newborn Self-Attachment Needs*. (unpublished paper) 1105 North Ontare, Santa Barbara, Ca 93105.

Coalition for Improving Maternity Services. (1996). International Journal of Childbirth Education 13(2): 26–28.

Cohen, B.B. (1993). *Sensing, Feeling, and Action*. Contact Editions. Northhampton, MA.

Eisenberg, L. (1995). *The Social Construction of the Human Brain*. American Journal of Psychiatry 152:11, 1563–1575.

Fonagy, P. (1999). *Attachment, The Holocaust, and The Outcome of Child Psyhchoanalysis: An Attachment-Based Model of Transgenerational Transmission of Trauma*. Sophia Mirviss Memorial Lecture, San Francisco Psychoanalytic Institute and Society, Child Development Program. February, 7, 1999, San Francisco, Ca.

Grey, K. (1992). *Creating the Environment for the Infant / Toddler's Capacity to Experience Mastery and Competence of His Abilities*. Student Handbook, Center for Child and Family Studies, Department of Human and Community Development, University of California, Davis.

Gunner, M.R., Brodersen, L., Krueger, K. & Rigatuso, R. (1996). *Dampening of behavioral and adrenocortical reactivity during early infancy: Normative changes and individual differences.* Child Development, 67:877–889.

Hoffman, J., Popbla, L., & Duhalde, C. (1998). *Early Stages of Initiative and Environmental Response.* Infant Mental Health Journal, 19(4), 355–377.

Horner, A. (1982) *Object Relations and the Developing Ego in Therapy.* New York: Jason Aronson.

Kennell, J.H. & Klaus, M. (1998). Bonding: Recent Obsrvations That Alter Perinatal Care. Pediatrics in Review, 19: 1, 4–12.

Klaus, M. & Klaus, P. (1998). *Your Amazing Newborn.* Perseus Books: Reading, Massachusetts.

Kovach, AC. (1996). *An Assessment Tool for Evaluating Hospital Breast-feeding Policies and Practices.* Journal of Human Lactation, 12(1): 41–5.

Lieberman, A. (1998). *An Infant Mental Health Perspective.* Zero to Three. December 1997/January 1998: 3–5.

Mahler, M.S., Pine, F., & Bergman, A. (1975). *The Psychological Birth of the Human Infant.* New York: Basic Books.

McDougall, J. (1989). *Theaters of the Body.* W.W. Norton & Company. New York.

Milner, B., Squire, L.R., & Kandel, E.R. (1998). *Cognitive Neuroscience and the Study of Memory.* Neuron, 20: 445–468.

Moberly, E.R. (1985). *The Psychology of Self and Other.* New York: Tavistock Publications.

Perry, B., Pollard, R., Blakeley, R., Baker, W., & Vigilante, D. (1995). *Childhood trauma, the neurobiology of adaptation, and "Usedependent" development of the Brain: How "states" become "traits".* Infant Mental Health Journal, 16(4) 271–289.

Reiner, R. (1997). *The First Years Last Forever. I Am Your Child.* Publication from the Reiner Foundation. Families and Work Institute. New York, N.Y.

Righard, L. & Adale, M. (1990). *Effects of Delivery Room Routines on Success Of First Breast-feed.* The Lancet, 336: 1105–07.

Robinson, J., Emde, R., & Korfmacher, J. (1997). *Integrating an Emotional Regulation Perspective in a Program of Prenatal and Early Childhood Home Visitation.* Journal of Community Psyhhology, 25(1) 59–75.

Schecter, D. (1980). Early Developmental Roots of Anxiety. Journal of the American Academy of Psychoanalysis 8:539–554.

Schore, A.N. (1994). *Affect Regulation and the Origin of the Self: The Neurobiology of Emotional Development.* Hillsdale, NJ: Erlbaum.

Settlage, C., Bemesderfer, S., Rosenthal, J., Afterman, J., & Spielman, P. (1991). *The Appeal Cycle in Early Mother-child Interaction: Nature and Implications of a Finding from Developmental Research.* The Journal of the American Psychoanalytic Association, 39:987–1015.

Shore, R. (1997). *Rethinking the Brain.* Families and Work Institute. New York, N.Y.

Siegel, D. (1996). *Cognition, Memory, and Dissociation.* Child and Adolescent Clinics of North America, 5:509–536.

Siegel, D. (1998). *The Developing Mind: Toward a Neurobiology of Interpersonal Experience.* The Signal, Newsletter of the World Association for Infant Mental Health 6, 3–4:1–11.

Stern, D.N. (1985). *The Interpersonal World of the Infant.* New York: Basic Books.

Stern, D.N. (1995). *The Motherhood Constellation.* New York: Basic Books.

Thoenen, H. (1995). *Neurotrophins and Neuronal Plasticity.* Science, 270, 593–598.

Tronick, E. (1989). Emotions and Emotional Communicationin Infants. American Psychologist, 44(2): 112–119.

Zero to Three/National Center for Clinical Infant Programs. (1994). *Diagnostic Classification of Mental Health and Developmental Disorders of Infancy and Early Childhood.* Zero to Three/National Center for Clinical Infant Programs, Arlington, Virginia.

Journal of Prenatal and Perinatal Psychology and Health, 13(3–4), Spring/Summer 1999

The Effects of Domestic Abuse on the Unborn Child

Amy L. Gilliland, B.A. and Thomas R. Verny, M.D., D Psych, FRCP(C)

ABSTRACT: This paper explores the relationship of domestic violence toward a pregnant mother on the subsequent behavior of her child. Through examination of the literature on physical abuse during pregnancy a picture emerges of the fetal environment. Exposure to this environment was consistently shown to have detrimental effects in infancy and childhood and in later adult life particularly evidenced by emotional and behavioral disorders, and increased evidence of criminal and violent behavior and suicide.

INTRODUCTION

In recent years, the issue of domestic violence has received much attention in scientific literature. While violence against women has been pervasive throughout human history, it is only recently that Western society openly rejected this behavior and created preventive laws. Domestic violence has several components which increase in severity over time. Verbal abuse, emotional abuse, physical abuse and sexual abuse occur in a specific order that are all designed to gain control of the victim by the perpetrator. It is characterized by a pattern of control, coercion, and assaults that an adult or an adolescent, most frequently male, uses to dominate or force compliance from a partner or spouse. (Helton, McFarlane, & Anderson, 1987).

Studies report that 7% (Helton, et al., 1987; McGrath, et al., 1991) to 17% (McFarlane, et al., 1992; Gazmararian, et al., 1996; Parker, et

Amy Gilliland, B.A. is a doula and associate of Alternative Birth Service, 1526 Vilas Ave., Madison, WI 53711-2226. Thomas R. Verny, MD, D Psych, FRCP(C) is the founder of APPPAH. He is considered one of the world's leading authorities on pre- and perinatal psychology. This paper is the result of research under his direction during the course of study in pre- and perinatal psychology he pioneered in conjunction with the Department of Human Development, Prenatal and Perinatal Psychology Program, St. Mary's University, Minneapolis. He may be contacted at 36 Madison Ave., Toronto, Ontario M5R251, Canada.

al., 1993) of pregnant women are currently in abusive relationships, and 21%–30% (Helton, et al., 1987) of all women have been abused at some point. Detailed personal interviews and interviews done later in pregnancy show even higher prevalence rates of such abuse (Petersen, et al., 1997). During pregnancy, physical assault is more likely to begin or escalate (DHHS Publication PHS 91-500212). A review of the literature shows clearly what the physical and emotional effects are on the pregnant woman and the neonate. Because the unborn child experiences everything the mother experiences, i.e. yelling voices, and physical and emotional trauma, he or she will be affected on every level—physiologically and psychologically. These data suggest that the majority of children of abused mothers will exhibit higher than normal levels of emotional disturbance or aggressive behavior.

THE GENESIS OF VIOLENCE AND ABUSE

Battering relationships start out magically. The abuser-to-be is romantic, thoughtful, and attentive. For the first several months or year, he is like a dream come true—whatever the woman has been looking for in a partner. Abusive behavior starts slowly, so that a woman's belief about her partner formed in these early months is not easily confronted. Abusers begin the mistreatment with sleep deprivation, interruption of eating patterns, complaints about the victim's worthlessness and faults, isolation from family and friends, and control over her finances. The perpetrator will have terrorizing rages that can erupt at any moment without warning. He may threaten the things she loves or destroy them. After a pattern of verbal and emotional abuse has been established and accepted by the victim, physical assault begins to occur. Women may be hit, slapped, punched, kicked, burned or injured with knives and guns. Sexual abuse begins after physical abuse. The women is forced to participate in sexual acts that she objects to, which further her feelings of shame and degradation (Brown, 1997). Sexual abuse is almost always accompanied by physical abuse. In the first study to make this association, sexual abuse is highly correlated with a risk of homicide or being killed by the abuser (McFarlane, 1998).

Pregnant women who are abused before pregnancy are likely to continue to be abused during the pregnancy. In fact, of women assaulted during pregnancy, 21%–33% report an increase in violence during that period (Campbell, et al., 1992; Stewart & Cecutti, 1993; etc.). Only a small minority of women, 3% reported a decrease in physical violence during the pregnancy (Amaro, et al., 1990).

EFFECTS OF DOMESTIC ABUSE ON THE PREGNANT WOMAN

Victims of violence were at greater risk of experiencing depression, attempting suicide, reported less happiness about being pregnant, and received less emotional support from others during the pregnancy. The pregnancy is more likely to be unintended (Gazmararian et al., 1995). Comparisons of victims and non-victims shows that victims are more likely to be users of alcohol, illegal and prescription drugs, and to smoke cigarettes during pregnancy (Amaro, et al., 1990; Stewart & Cecutti, 1993; Webster, et al., 1996).

One study showed that abused women are more likely to have epilepsy and asthma, have a higher incidence of miscarriage, two or more pregnancy terminations, and experienced a neonatal death (Webster, et al., 1996).

Consequences of physical abuse include abdominal trauma resulting in placental abruption, fetal death independent of the abruption, preterm labor and delivery, direct fetal injury, and fetomaternal hemorrhage. Maternal complications include hypovolemic shock, and rupture of the uterus, spleen and liver (Petersen, et al., 1997; McDonald, 1968).

Carlson, Gielen, and O'Campo (1994) found that moderate or severe violence is experienced in the postpartum period by 41% of the women who had been abused prenatally. Moreover, 17% of the women who were not abused during the pregnancy reported moderate to severe physical abuse postpartum.

It seems obvious to assume that women who are victims of domestic violence experience a great deal of distress in their lives. They more commonly experience higher levels of anxiety, depression and demoralization (Petersen, et al., 1997). Battered women are more than twice as likely as non-battered women to experience emotional problems, job loss, legal problems, and parenting problems. They were 20% more likely to have experienced undesirable life changes and the added stress of the death of a friend or family member (Bullock & McFarlane, 1989).

THE EFFECTS OF MATERNAL ANXIETY ON BIRTH

Numerous studies have reported on the levels of maternal anxiety and its effects on the birth process and the neonate (Ferreira, 1960;

Istvan, 1986; Carlson, 1979; Farber, 1981; Field, et al., 1985; Van Den Bergh, 1990). In a summary of studies of perinatal complications the strongest associated factor was occurrence of recent stressful life events (Paykel ES, Emms EM, et al., 1980). Nuckolls found that women who had high life change scores both prior to and during pregnancy were twice as susceptible to pregnancy complications if their test scores indicated the presence of psychosocial liabilities rather than assets (Nuckolls, et al., 1972).

Gorsuch and Key (1974) found the pregnancy and birth complications were positively associated with high to average levels of state anxiety in the third and fourth months of pregnancy and also with life change in the second and third trimesters of pregnancy. They also found that contemporary life experiences seemed more important than past events in predicting reproductive outcome. McDonald and Parham (1964) found that birth complications were more likely to occur with women who tested as using "denial, rationalization, and sublimation defenses to deal with their feelings." These women "emphasized strength through power and aggression". In a review of the literature, the main findings were that patients with obstetric complications had higher anxiety levels than women with normal gestations and deliveries (Istvan, 1986).

An association of domestic violence with low birth weight of infants was found in four studies (Bullock & McFarlane, 1989; Webster, et al., 1996; Parker & McFarlane, et al., 1993; Petersen, et al., 1997). Also, mothers who experience high levels of anxiety gave birth to infants of lower birth weights. The incidence of life changes and current nature of the abusive relationship seems to have an effect on the anxiety level of the mother, which might correlate with the low birth weight. The effect was ameliorated when the abused mother had a high level of social support (McLean, et al., 1993). However most abused women lacked social connection with others.

Maternal anxiety and significant life stress has also been shown to correlate with premature birth (McDonald, 1968).

PHYSIOLOGICAL EFFECTS ON THE FETUS

Women assaulted during pregnancy are more likely to experience preterm labor even if it does not directly follow a physical attack. They are also more prone to chorioamnionitis. This condition is associated with sexually transmitted diseases which tend to accompany illicit drug use (Berenson, et al., 1994). Several possible indirect physiological consequences have been noted. Myers (1975), in experiments with rhesus monkeys, argued that neuroendocrines released as part of the stress response to exposure to adverse events, particularly epinephrine and norepinephrine, tend to reduce uterine blood flow, resulting in fetal hypoxia. Other laboratory experiments have demonstrated that exposure to stressors is associated with increases of catecholamine secretion and reports of increased anxiety. The increased catecholamines in the mother's system whenever she was verbally, emotionally, physically or sexually abused would be an unusual effect on the fetus's uterine environment.

As Carlson (1979) points out, in a literature review of maternal emotionality and reproductive outcome, "the duration and intensity of the stress" are probably among the most critical factors. It seems likely that continuation of the stress situation affects reproduction via chronic overactivity of the adrenocortical system and ultimately results in a reduction of the organism's ability to cope adequately. Although Carlson's article did not specifically examine domestic violence, the situation described seems to fit that of the chronically battered woman and her unborn baby.

Maternal anxiety scores, both trait anxiety and state anxiety, were positively correlated with fetal behavior and movement and neonatal behavior and movement by Van Den Bergh (1990). So there is a high correlation between the baby's movements and behavior both before and after birth due to anxiety in the mother. Babies born to the more anxious mothers had more gastrointestinal problems, cried more frequently, and were perceived as having a difficult temperament. The anxious women also had more pregnancy and delivery complications.

Farber (1981) examined anxious mothers and found that mother-infant interaction differed when compared with non-anxious mothers, but only with female infants. However Farber only gave one anxiety scale test during the third trimester, while Van Den Bergh (1990) gave seven test batteries, and also tested during each trimester. Gorsuch and Key (1974) found that testing close to the stressful or anxious event made a difference in their results. The timing of the test seems to be important in ascertaining whether there is an anxiety effect.

Reduced fetal activity and increased neonatal activity is also shown as a result of maternal anxiety in primiparous women. Mothers with less anxiety experienced fewer obstetrical complications, had higher birth weight infants, and their infants performed better on the Brazelton neonatal behavior assessment scale. These neonates were also less irritable and less active after birth (Field, et al., 1985).

A relationship has also been shown between pre-eclampsia, also known as toxemia, and maternal anxiety. In 1963, Glick and others interviewed 40 patients who had previously experienced toxemia. There may also be a direct relationship between continued exposure to distressing situations and pre-eclampsia. As mentioned previously, women exposed to stress were more likely to produce increased catecholoamines in response. Noradrenaline, one of the main catecholamines, has been shown to have a major role in the development of pre-eclampsia. Since abused women are exposed to repeated violating events, it is possible that they are at higher risk for pre-eclampsia (Manyonda, Slater, et al., 1998). The women who later developed the condition in a subsequent pregnancy were more likely to be single, or become separated, divorced or widowed during pregnancy. They were more likely to be habitual aborters or to be characterized as "accident prone". Domestic violence victims were frequently assessed as "accident prone" in medical records because of the shame and stigma associated with wifebeating 35 years ago when this study was done. Separation, divorce or the death of a spouse rank as one of the highest anxiety producers on the life stress index (Barnett, Hanna, et al., 1983). These women are also shown to be habitual aborters (Webster, et al., 1996). The consequences to the mother of high stress events such as habitual abortions, and "accident proneness" are similar to the effects of domestic violence on its victims.

EFFECTS ON THE PERSONALITY OF THE UNBORN CHILD

According to Garbarino, Guttmand and Sealey (1986), psychological maltreatment is a concerted attack by an adult on a child's development of self and social psychologically destructive behavior, and takes five forms. Utilizing this formulation, the prenatal effects of the five types of abuse may also be observed. The first category of abuse is *rejecting*. The adult refuses "to acknowledge the child's worth and the legitimacy of the child's needs." In the prenatal period, this would include not allowing the child's mother to have adequate rest and food. Unwanted and mistimed pregnancies account for over 70% of babies conceived by domestic violence victims while for non-abused women, the figure is 43% (Gazmararian, Adams, et al., 1995). Rejecting the pregnancy and anger at the conception is common for most abusers. They are likely to psychologically reject the child and may even accuse the mother of conceiving the baby by someone else.

The second form of mistreatment is *isolating*. The adult separates the child from normal social experiences, prevents the child from forming friendships, and makes the child believe that he or she is alone in the world. By segregating the mother from social contact with other pregnant women, the abuser also isolates the child. By physically and emotionally abusing the mother and creating stress and anxiety, the child's primitive system is bathed in catecholamines. The physical stress system of the mother detaches the child from her in vital ways. The mother's emotional stress and her focus on the needs of her attacker, rather than the unborn child, also alienates the pregnant women from her fetus—even though they occupy the same body.

The third form of harassment is *terrorizing*. "The adult verbally assaults the child, creates a climate of fear, bullies and frightens the child, and makes the child believe that the world is capricious and hostile." By yelling at the unborn baby, calling it names and rejecting it as his own, the abuser frightens the fetal child. The frequent verbal and sometimes physical attacks are scary and possibly terrorizing. When those attacks are mixed in with periods of affection, the unpredictability of mood may be even more overwhelming for the prenate, than they are for the mother.

The fourth form of misuse is *ignoring*. "The adult deprives the child of essential stimulation and responsiveness, stifling emotional growth and intellectual development." The basic emotional and intellectual needs of the unborn have not been clearly defined. However it has been shown that music, language programs, and other forms of stimulation affect children's intellectual and behavioral capacity beyond the usual (Blum, 1993). By not allowing the basic conditions of a quiet, peaceful environment, and security in the emotional caretaking abilities of his parents, the baby is deprived and his needs ignored.

The fifth form of negativity is *corrupting*. "The adult stimulates the child to engage in destructive antisocial behavior, reinforces that deviance, and makes the child unfit for normal social experience." The whole environment for the unborn child of a battered woman is toxic. The child lives in a world of imminent physiological stress, bathed in more stress hormones than usual. The vocative environment is one of loud voices, yelling, the sounds of slapping and possible physiological pain. The feeling states of the mother are communicated to the child, along with the probable feeling of being unwanted. Nine months in such a toxic environment may create a child who is unfit for normal social experience, and who will grow to engage in self destructive or antisocial behavior.

LONG TERM EFFECTS OF DOMESTIC VIOLENCE ON THE UNBORN

Children gestates under conditions of domestic abuse are more likely to have emotional disorders, commit violent crimes and kill themselves. Mothers found to be highly anxious during pregnancy were found to exert more control over their children and to parent in an authoritarian manner. They reveal greater dissatisfaction with the role of being a mother and evidence more marital conflict and irritability in relations with their children and partners. Children tended to receive lower developmental quotients in both the mental and motor areas and, in general, present a less favorable picture of emotional adjustment (Davids, Holden & Gray, 1963).

The mother's perception of her child as an infant has a significant impact on that child's later development. Mothers who were noted prenatally to have poor self-esteem, lack of confidence in themselves as mothers, and view their environmental support systems as less helpful, reported more trouble in caring for their infants and often seem depressed and anxious. All other factors of the baby's behavior and health being equal, these infants were considered to be high risk, at one month of age, based solely on their mother's perception of them. At 4–5 years of age and 10–11 years of age, significantly more children who were originally classified high risk as infants were diagnosed as having an emotional or psychosocial disorders (Broussard, 1979). The qualities associated with pregnant women who are in abusive relationships are also associated with infants at high risk of an emotional or psychosocial disorder later in life. Batchelor, et al., (1991) found emotional and behavioral disorders in children correlated highly with certain prenatal risk factors. Younger maternal age, more cigarettes smoked, prior problem pregnancies, increased maternal stress during pregnancy, increased use of medication during pregnancy, and lower birth weight of the infant correlated with emotional disturbance in the child. When these factors were present, a child was 2.5 times more likely to have a behavioral disturbance. Emotionally disturbed children also showed a higher frequency of most perinatal complications.

This is the *same* list of factors that correlate with physical domestic abuse during pregnancy. In one study, Kandel and Mednick (1991), found that 80% percent of violent offenders in their prospective case controlled study had experienced complications at birth. Only 8.5% of the whole group who experienced complications at birth committed a violent crime. But 80% of the group who were violent offenders had experienced a major birth complication. No pregnancy risk factors experienced by domestic violence victims were tested for individually in this study.

Raine, Brennan and Mednick (1994), found a high correlation between maternal rejection and birth complications. Ninety percent of the male group experiencing both factors committed violent offenses before the age of 18 years. Maternal rejection was defined by the mother's negative attitude to pregnancy and either attempted abortion or institutionalization of the child by the mother.

Jacobson and Bygdeman (1998), discovered in their case control study that birth complications and use of interventions are associated with an increased risk of suicide by violent means by adult men. For multiple birth trauma, the infant is 4.9 times more likely to commit suicide as an adult. Suicides by non-violent means were not included in this study. The other evidence for suicide by male youth is less direct. Of those committing suicide, 25–40% are known to have personality disorders, and 25%–75% are known to have emotional disorders (Hollinger, et al., 1994). Emotional disorders that are implicated in those experiencing birth complications, correlated with emotional conditions of the mother are the same as those experienced by domestic violence victims.

CONCLUSION

Domestic violence is a horrific experience for victims who are entrenched in the cycle of abusive behavior. Unborn children, trapped in their mother's wombs, are also victims. Mothers are more likely to smoke, use alcohol, prescription and illicit drugs as a coping mechanism for the abuse. Their sleep and nutrition is more likely to be poor, and they may have aborted one or more babies before this one was conceived. The unborn child may experience direct physical trauma from the father's blows to the abdomen. Because of the emotional stress of arguments and fear of abuse, the mother's body creates more stress hormones more often than normal and the baby is bathed in adrenaline and noradrenaline. This becomes a part of the child's normal experience of living.

Mothers are more likely to be anxious and stressed, which has been shown to correlate with pregnancy complications, birth complications, pre-eclampsia, premature labor and birth, low birth weight, and infection of the amniotic membrane. Because of the stress hormones, the fetus receives less blood volume which carry nutrients and oxygen. Ultimately, the mother's whole body can become toxic and go into shock, resulting in the death of the mother and baby if not treated. Pre-eclampsia or toxemia is associated with maternal anxiety, domestic abuse during pregnancy, and overstimulation of stress hormones. Babies, in turn, are more likely to be irritable, cry more often, exhibit motor and learning difficulties, perform less well on the Brazelton scale, and have gastrointestinal problems.

Battering during pregnancy is associated with emotional and behavioral disorders during childhood and severe psychological problems later in life. These children are truly at risk even before emerging from the birth canal.

REFERENCES

Amaro, H., Fried, L. E., et al. (1990). *Violence during Pregnancy and Substance Use.* American Journal of Public Health, Vol 80(5), 575–579.

Barnett, B., Hanna, B., et al. (1983). *Life Event Scales for Obstetric Groups.* Journal of Psychomatic Research, Vol. 27(4), 313–320.

Batchelor, E. S., Dean, R. S., Gray, J. W., et al. (1991). *Classification Rates and relative risk factos for perinatal events predicting emotional behavioral disorders in children.* Pre and Perinatal Psychology Journal, Vol. 5(4), 327–341.

Berenson, A., Wiemann, C., et al. (1994). *Perinatal morbidity associated with violence experienced by pregnant women.* American Journal of Obstetrics and Gynecology, Vol. 170(6), 1760–1769.

Blum, T. (1993). *Prenatal Perception, Learning and Bonding.* Leonardo Publishers, Hong Kong.

Broussard, E. (1979). *Assessment of the adaptive potential of the mother-infant system: the neonatal perception inventories.* Seminars in Perinatology, Vol. 3(1), 91–100.

Brown, Lou. (1997). *Stop Domestic Violence: An Action Plan for Saving Lives.* New York: St. Martin's Press. This description is based on Brown's accounts.

Bullock, L. F., McFarlane, J. (1989). *The birth-weight battering connection.* American Journal of Nursing, Sept 1989, 89, 1153–1155.

Bullock, L. F., McFarlane, J. (1989). *The Prevalence and characteristics of battered women in a primary care setting.* Nurse Practioner, June 1989, 47–55.

Campbell, J. C., Poland, M. L., Waller, J. B., et al. (1992). *Correlates of Battering during Pregnancy.* Research in Nursing and Health, Vol. 15, 219–226.

Carlson, D., & LaBarba, R. (1979). *Maternal Emotionality during pregnancy and reproductive outcome: a review of the literature.* International Journal of Behavioral Development (2), 343–376.

Davids, A., Holden, R., & Gray, G. (1963). *Maternal Anxiety during pregnancy and adequacy of mother and child adjustment, eight months following childbirth.* Child Development, Vol. 34, 993–1002.

Farber, E., Vaughn, B., & Egeland, B. (1981). *The relationship of prenatal maternal anxiety to infant behavior and mother-infant interaction during the first six months of life.* Early Human Development, Vol. 5, 267–277.

Ferreira, A. J. (1960). *The pregnant woman's emotional attitude and its reflection on the newborn.* American Journal of Orthopsychiatry, Vol. 30, 553–561.

Field, T., Sandburg, D., et al. (1985). *Effects of ultrasound feedback on pregnancy anxiety, fetal activity, and neonatal outcome.* Obstetrics and Gynecology, Vol. 66(4), 525–527.

Garbarino, J., Guttmann, D., & Seeley, J. (1986). *The Psychologically Battered Child.* Jossey–Bass, San Francisco.

Gazmararian JA, Adams MM, et al. (1995) *Relationship between pregnancy intendedness and physical violence in mothers of newborns.* Obstetrics and Gynecology, Vol. 85(6), 1031–38.

Gazmararian, J. A., Lazorick, S., et al. (1996). *Prevalence of Violence Against Pregnant Women.* JAMA, Vol. 275(24), 1915–1920.

Geilen, A. C., O'Campo, P., et al. (1994). *Interpersonal Conflict and Physical Violence during the childbearing year.* Social Science Medicine, Vol. 39(6), 781–787.

Gorsuch, R. L., & Key, M. K. (1974). *Abnormalities of pregnancy as a function of anxiety and life stress.* Psychosomatic Medicine, 36, 352–362.

Hollinger, P., Offer, D., et al. (1994). *Suicide and Homicide Among Adolescents.* Guilford Press: New York.

Helton, A., McFarlane, J., & Anderson, E. (1987). *Battered and pregnant. —A prevalence study.* American Journal of Public Health, 77, 1337–1339.

Istvan, J. (1986). *Stress, anxiety, and birth outcomes: a critical review of the evidence.* American Psychological Bulletin, Vol. 100(3), 331–348.

Jacobson, B., & Bygdeman, M. (1998). *Obstetric care and proneness of offspring to suicide as adults: case control study.* British Medical Journal, Vol. 317, 1346–1349.

Kandel, E., & Mednick, S. (1991). *Perinatal complication predict violent offending.* Criminology, Vol. 29(3), 519–5.

Manyonda, I. T., Slater, D., et al. (1998) *A role for noradrenaline in pre-eclampsia: towards a unifying hypothesis for the pathophysiology.* British Journal of Obstetrics and Gynecology, Vol. 105, 641–648.

McGrath, M. E., Hogan, J. W., & Peipert, J. F. (1991). *A Prevalence Survey of Abuse and Screening for Abuse in Urgent Care Patients.* Obstetrics and Gynecology, 91(4), 511–514.

McDonald, R. L., & Parham, K. J. (1964). *Relation of emotional changes during pregnancy to obstetric complications in unmarried primigravidas.* American Journal of Obstetrics and Gynecology, Vol. 90, 195–201.

McDonald, R. (1968). *The role of emotional factors in obstetric complications: a review.* Psychosomatic Medicine, 30, 222–237.

McFarlane, J., Wiist, W., & Watson, M. (1998). *Characteristics of Sexual Abuse against Pregnant Hispanic Women by Their Male Intimates.* Journal of Women's Health, Vol. 7(6), 1998, 739–745.

McFarlane, J., Parker, B., Soeken, K., & Bullock, L. (1992). *Assessing for Abuse During Pregnancy.* JAMA, 267(23), 3176–3178.

McLean, D. E., Hatfield-Timajchy, K., et al. (1993). *Psychosocial measurement: implications for the study of preterm delivery in black women.* American Journal of Preventitive Medicine, 1993:ps, 39–81.

Meyrs, R. E. (1975). *Maternal Psychological Stress and Fetal Asphyxia: a study in the monkey.* American Journal of Obstetrics and Gynecology, Vol. 122, 47–59.

Nuckolls, K. B., Cassel, J., & Kaplan, B. H. (1972). *Psychosocial assets, life crisis, and the prognosis of pregnancy.* Americal Journal of Epidemiology, Vol. 95, 431–441.

Parker, B., McFarlane, J., et al. (1993). *Physical and Emotional Abuse in Pregnancy: A Comparison of Adult and Teenage Women.* Nursing Research, Vol. 42(3), 173–178.

Petersen, R., Gazmararian, J., Spitz, A., et al. (1997). *Violence and Adverse Pregnancy Outcomes: A Review of the Literature and Directions for Future Research.* American Journal of Preventative Medicine, Vol. 13(5), 366–373.

Paykel, E. S., Emms, E. M., et al. (1980). *Life events and social support in puerperal depression.* British Journal of Psychiatry, 136, 339–346.

Raine, A., Brennan, P., & Mednick, S. (1994). *Birth complications combined with early maternal rejection at age 1 year predispose to violent crime at age 18 years.* Archives of General Psychiatry, Vol. 51, 984–988.

Stewart, D. E., & Cecutti, A. (1993). *Physical Abuse in Pregnancy.* CMAJ: Canadian Medical Association Journal, 149(9), 1257–1263.

U. S. Department of Health and Human Services. (1990). *Healthy people 2000: National health promotion and disease prevention objectives* (DHHS Publication PHS 91-500212). Washington, DC.

Van Den Bergh, B. (1990). *The influence of maternal emotions during pregnancy on fetal and neonatal behavior.* Pre and Perinatal Psychology, 5(2), 119–130.

Webster, J., Chandler, J., & Battistutta, D. (1996). *Pregnancy Outcomes and health care use: Effects of abuse.* American Journal of Obstetrics and Gynecology, Vol 174(2), 760–767.

ADDITIONAL REFERENCES

Connolly, A., Katz, V., et al. (1997). *Trauma in Pregnancy.* American Journal of Perinatology, Vol. 14(6), 331–336.

Dutton, M. (1992). *Empowering and Healing the Battered Woman.* Springer Publishing Company, New York.

Evans, P. (1992). *The Verbally Abusive Relationship.* Bob Adams, Inc., Massachusetts.

Freeman, J. (1985). *Prenatal and Perinatal Factors Associated with Brain Disorders.* NIH 85-1149.

Nijhuis, J. G., Prechtel, H. F., et al. (1982). *Are there Behavioral States in the Human Fetus.* Early Human Development, Vol. 6, 177–195.

Raine, A., Venables, P. H., et al. (1990). *Relationships between central and autonomic measures of arousal at age 15 years and criminality at age 24 years.* Archives of General Psychiatry, Vol. 47, 1003–1007.

Walling, M. K., Reiter, R., et al. (1994). *Abuse history and chronic pain in woman: Prevalences of sexual abuse and physical abuse.* Obstetrics and Gynecology, Vol. 84(2), 193–199.

Widom, C. (1989). *The cycle of violence.* Science, Vol. 244, 160–166.

Journal of Prenatal and Perinatal Psychology and Health, 13(3–4), Spring/Summer 1999

Antecedents to Somatoform Disorders: A Pre- and Perinatal Psychology Hypothesis

Bobbi J. Lyman, M.A.

ABSTRACT: The somatoform cluster of behavioral disorders is the single most frequent class of unexplainable problems found in primary care medical settings today. What is known about these disorders is that there are physiological, social, and psychological variables that need to be considered. What is not known is how a person develops a propensity toward having physical symptoms as their primary complaint. The author suggests that human beings are classically conditioned when faced with intolerable emotional experiences in the womb or during birth. The residual feelings are laid down in the developing brain's neural pathways in an adaptive strategy of escape and avoidance (focusing on the body instead of the feelings), allowing the organism to survive.

INTRODUCTION

Somatization has been defined the most simply and intelligibly as: The expression of psychological pain through physical symptoms (Fauman, 1994). Physical pain is defined here as an unpleasant sensory experience that is associated with actual tissue damage (Benoliel, 1995). The somatoform disorders, according to the DSM-IV (*Diagnostic and Statistical Manual of Mental Disorders*; APA, 1994), are a cluster of symptoms and behaviors with common features, primarily persistent or recurring physical complaints that are not supported by actual physical findings (Kirmayer & Taillefer, 1997).

The somatoform cluster of behavioral disorders are the single most frequent class of problems in primary care medical settings (Mayou, Bass & Sharpe, 1995). Unexplained symptoms constitute from 25% to 60% of family medicine practices (Kirkwood, Clure, et al., 1982). These disorders cause clinically significant personal distress and/or impairments in social, occupational, or other areas of functioning (APA, 1994). Though the focus may be on bodily ailments, the research

Bobbi J. Lyman, M.A., is a Clinical Psychology Doctoral Student at the The Fielding Institute. She may be contacted at 3202 Pine Road, Bremerton, WA 98310. Email: bjlyman@telebyte.com

247

shows, there are also many more complex, underlying psychosocial and emotional antecedents, pain-related dysfunctions or disabilities, comorbid conditions, and pain-sustaining factors as well (Reid, Balis & Sutton, 1997).

PSYCHOSOCIAL ANTECEDENTS

The concept that psychosocial stressors influence or exacerbate illness is certainly not new. Clinicians know that it is often possible to understand the complexity of present difficulties by examining the individual's life history. Many studies have noted that traumatic or stressful experiences seem to be qualitatively different from memories of ordinary events and are more emotional in nature (Teff, 1988; van der Kolk, 1994). Elevated life stress predicts a greater frequency of medical visits, strongest among patients with personality traits characterizing a tendency toward somatization (Miranda, Perez-Stable, Munoz, Hargreaves & Henke, 1991).

It is a very difficult task determining the underlying components when diagnosing and treating a somatoform disorder because of the multitude of psychological factors that may contribute to the development, maintenance, or exacerbation of a somatic or physical complaint. Adding to the confusion is uncertainty as to the antecedents of the psychological pain. There are divergent views from scientists on this issue of origination as well. Before looking more closely at the hypothesis offered as an explanation of the antecedents, found in the earliest period of human development, an examination of the *expression* of physical complaints, within a cultural context will be offered.

PAIN EXPRESSION AND CULTURE

Every culture determines what are the accepted "help-seeking" behaviors for emotional pain and human suffering. If physical complaints are more socially acceptable than psychological distress, as is true in the United States, then somatic complaints are expressed (Chaplin, 1997). Western culture allows symptom relief when received from a physician who can determine the source of the pain or complaint and prescribe the appropriate medication. The cultural norm for pain expression in the United States is that a person will be given sympathy and attention with a physical ailment but can expect rejection with a mental one.

UNDERLYING EMOTIONAL ANTECEDENTS

Because all people in the U. S. who are subjected to this same socialization process do not have a physical symptom focus, we need to look still deeper. There is general acknowledgment among professional therapists that affect regulation and biological patternings are closely related (Schore, 1994; LeDoux, 1993; Thayer, 1989). This would seem intuitively correct as emotions give human beings a distinctive readiness to act. LeDoux (1993), for example, has looked at precisely this *emotion-to-action* question within the amygdala (limbic system) in the architecture of the brain. His research found that *inputting* sensory signals travel into the brain to the thalamus first (previously known), then across a single synapse to the amygdala, giving it the ability to begin to respond first (previously unknown) before the cerebral cortex does. This is essentially saying that the amygdala is ready to act when the thinking brain is still coming to a decision on how to respond.

The role of the emotions in psychological development has been studied substantially. Currently there are detailed descriptors on how each emotion prepares the body for a very different kind of response (Goleman, 1995). In fact, anxiety can actually produce physical pain when the prolonged muscle tension associated with anxiety may trigger other points and induce vasoconstriction (Carlson, 1995).

THEORY AND RESEARCH AROUND PAIN

In the last several decades there has been a swing from the entirely mechanistic biological view to a complexity that includes individual, environmental, and cultural characteristics. An article of this length can not cover the advances in theory in all these areas adequately, so two specific views will be looked at around physical pain symptoms:

1) where emotions are a factor, and
2) from an evolutionary perspective where survival is the motivator.

EMOTIONS

In the last 15–20 years, a number of new theories on the nature of emotion have been proposed (Bower, 1981; Lang, 1984; Leventhal,

1984) and attempts at investigating and explaining emotionally-driven behaviors have appeared (Leventhal & Tomarken, 1986). These have shown relevance to somatoform pain behaviors in clinical treatment. For example promising research, such as the disclosure of emotions paradigm (Dominguez, et al., 1995) is helping to clarify the psychological variables that increases a patient's risk for developing a somatic pain problem. These patients are said to be psychologically *stuck* in the past with its consequential depression. Unless they express the emotion and focus on the present they remain past-focused and pain-prone. There is also literature which shows that the impact of any emotionally stressful event can be significantly influenced by how a person appraises the situation and/or copes with it (Gatchel, Baum, & Krantz, 1988). This in turn influences how individuals differ in their emotional and physiological responses. For example, one person may have an increased heart rate and blood pressure but no muscle tension, whereas another will have primarily increased muscle tension. The research examined the particular physiologic symptom or organ which was identified as more stressed. However, this systematic research has yet to determine the predictive validity of the vunerable organ becoming the future somatoform focus.

The diathesis-stress model of illness (Levi, 1974) proposed simply that psychosocial, environmental, genetic, and physiological elements should be considered interactive. A physiological predisposition toward a certain illness (genetic weakness or biochemical imbalance), psychosocial stimuli (stress and how a person responds to and copes with it), and previously experienced environmental conditions jointly determine many disease states. Animal research has supported a diathesis-stress model of various psychophysiological disorders (Gatchel, et al., 1988).

EVOLUTIONARY VIEW

An evolutionary perspective would say that physical symptoms and pain are a way the body signals something is wrong and that other activities should cease until the damage is stopped (Neese & Williams, 1994). Memory of a painful event, for example, teaches the individual to avoid the same situation in the future. Even when there is a medical condition such as an injury or surgery to remove an organ, the pain is adaptive because continued use of damaged tissue may compromise the effectiveness of the functional portions of the body that remain. Thus pain is fundamentally essential for survival.

Unpleasant emotions can be thought of as a defense analogous to pain from an evolutionary perspective. Just as the capacity for physical pain has evolved to protect human beings from tissue damage, the capacity for anxiety has emerged to protect us against future dangers and other kinds of threats. Another example of evolutionary protectiveness is our experience of fatigue to keep us from a state of overexertion. Evolutionary psychologists might say that to be able to respond to every situation and cope with the challenges of life, adaptive ways of functioning (e.g., internal psychological regulation based on past experiences) were necessary for human survival. In this capacity, pain clearly functions as a protective survival mechanism. However, evolutionary processes do not always follow a completely logical track. Consider that our immune system is able to recognize and attack a million foreign proteins, yet we still get pneumonia. Is a survival-oriented, yet perhaps unseen limit reached here also, as in fatigue?

What might happen when too much emotional pain is experienced which predictably could lead to a serious psychopathological state? If for example, an individual's early traumatic experiences were so overwhelming that a realization of them would make life appear unbearable, an individual might have another coping mechanism that would take the (emotional) overload completely out of the anxious state and into the physical body focus. A parallel illustration for this concept might be when a student recognizes that he/she is failing a course and feels anxious. Doesn't he/she tend to drop the class (not facing the failure which could be devastating) and try another subject (or even quit school)? Not failing is equated with emotional survival in this case. Withdrawing is the way that the pain of failing (not surviving) functions to limit an individual's range of responses, whether that is an intolerable emotional feeling, or a physically painful experiences. This makes sense clinically where somatoform patients are observed as having severe limits in their own capacity for absorbed attention, processing information, and goal-directed behaviors.

HYPOTHESIS OF A PRE- AND PERINATAL ANTECEDENT FOR SOMATOFORM PAIN COMPLAINTS

If the psychological components of the DSM-IV somatoform pain disorders emerge somehow from emotional stress or trauma in the absence of physical findings, how the affective antecedent is transformed into physical symptoms should be of interest to researchers attempting to learn about, and help, this difficult patient population. Returning to the evolutionary psychology viewpoint, the reason the emotional pain may become perceived physical pain is an adaptation of escape and avoidance from stress or trauma allowing the organism to survive. This transformation may occur through the process of classical conditioning where the early experience is extremely agonizing-often a life or death event. Kessler and his colleagues (1996) have stated that the effects of childhood adversities on later adult psychopathology are largely due to powerful effects at first onset rather than later events or conditioning. We also know neurophysiologically that bundles of nerves, connected together, learn by repeating highly emotive experiences (van der Kolk, 1989).

Researchers are calling for clarification of the antecedents of psychopathology, subjective emotional conditions and experiences, and physiological activity (Behavioral Science Task Force of the National Advisory Mental Health Council, 1995). It appears that the entrenched, but adaptive, somatoform behaviors originated and remain in the preverbal neural pathways laid down in the pre- and perinatal time frame of life. When taken in total with later reinforcing and socializing experiences, these illusive origins of later symptoms often remain unreachable to the clinician in the somatoform patient.

Emerson (1996) has indicated that the earliest (pre- and perinatal) "traumas shape how subsequent events will be perceived and experienced." Frank Lake (1987, 1981) also pointed to the period of gestation for the origin of somatoform complaints. According to Lake, psychosomatic equivalents of chronic resentment and hostility are early emotional states ("persecutory womb experiences") that produced high blood pressure, ulcerative colitis, asthma, rheumatoid arthritis, peptic ulcers, dermatitis, chronic colds or sinus infections, and chronic nasal congestion. Lake's supposition was that prenatal trauma is repressed and then transferred into other areas of the body until it later manifests in a dysfunction or disease.

The immediate critique to a pre- and perinatal psychology paradigm has been that for the most part psychologists do not believe the idea that people have the ability to retain early traumatic experiences (Bauer, 1996). The objections are based on the lack of solid evidence that early experiences are related to later mental processes and the general conviction that the preverbal brain is not sufficiently developed to record early experience (Riedlinger & Riedlinger, 1986). But hopefully, this view is becoming antiquated with the medical innovation of obstetrical monitoring devices (ultrasound and fiber optic cameras) that allow us to view prenates as active, and reactive (physically and emotionally) when they can be seen to strike out against the invasiveness of an amniocentesis needle. These new technologies are now added to the overwhelming evidence that the physical and sensory systems are functional during the preand perinatal time frarne. Further, with the addition of LeDoux's valuable research it has been shown that there is a functional neural pathway for fast-acting, emergency-type responses other than only through the cortex, as was previously thought.

As long as the antecedents of somatic pain complaints remain unknown, these patients remain difficult and costly to treat. What is known is that there are physiological, social, and psychological variables that need to be considered when treating these disorders. What is not known is what gives a person a propensity or premorbidity toward having physical pain as their primary symptom complaint. Human beings' emotional and physical defenses are the (primary) armament they have when they are at the earliest preverbal developmental stage of life. These sensory and bodily coping mechanisms that worked early on were laid down in the developing brain's neural pathways which-after cultural and environmental reinforcement, continue to direct the behaviors in the present. This behavior occurs over and over in the present when a classically conditioned emotional stressor is triggered by a life circumstance, The psychological stress factor reverberates through the system, then defaults to the physical pain focus, as it did originally. An everyday example of this is when a person pulls his/her hand away from a hot surface instinctively. This strategy is superior to taking the time to evaluate if it is in our best interest to withdraw.

REFERENCES

American Psychiatric Association. (1994). *Diagnostic and statistical manual of mental disorders* (4th ed.). Washington, D.C.: Author.

Bauer, P. J. (1996). What do infants recall of their lives? Memory for specific events by one- and two-year-olds. *American Psychologist, 51*(1), 29–41.

Behavioral Science Task Force of the National Advisory Mental Health Council (1995). Basic Behavioral Science Research for Mental Health: A National Investment: Emotion and Motivation. *American Psychologist, 50*(10), 838–845.

Benoliel, J. (1995). Multiple meanings of pain and complexities of pain management. *Nursing Clinics of North America, 30*(4), 583.

Bower, G. H. (1981). Mood and memory. *American Psychologist, 31,* 129–148.

Carlson, N. R. (1994). *Physiology of behavior.* Boston, MA: Allyn and Bacon.

Chaplin, S. L. (1997). Somatization. In W. Tseng & J. Streltzer (Eds.), *Culture & psychopathology: A guide to clinical assessment* (67–86). New York: Brunner/Mazel.

Dominguez, B., Valderrama, P., de los Angeles Meza, M., Perez, S. L., Silva, A., Martinez, G., Mendez, V. M. & Olvera, Y. (1995). The roles of disclosure and emotional reversal in clinical practice. In J.W. Pennebaker (ed.), *Emotion, disclosure, & health.* Washington, DC: American Psychological Association.

Emerson, W. R. (1996). The vulnerable prenate. *Pre- and Perinatal Psychology Journal,* 10(3), 125–142.

Fauman, M. A. (1994). *Study Guide to DSM-IV.* Washington, D.C.: American Psychiatric Press, Inc.

Gatchel, R. J., Baum, A., & Krantz, D. S. (1988). *An introduction to health psychology* (2 d ed.). New York: McGraw-Hill.

Goleman, D. (1995). *Emotional Intelligence.* New York: Bantam Books.

Kessler, R. C., Nelson, C. B., McGonagle, K. A., Lieu, J., Swartz, M., & Blazer, D. G. (1996). Comorbidity of DSM-111-R major depressive disorder in the general population: results from the U. S. National Comorbidity Survey. *British Journal of Psychiatry,* 169, 17–30.

Kirkwood, C. R., Clure, H. R., Brodsky, R., Gould, G. H., Knaak, R., Metcalf, M., & Romeo, S. (1982). The diagnostic content of family practice: 50 most common diagnoses recorded in the WAMI community practices. *Journal of Family Practice,* 15(3), 485–492.

Kirmayer, L. J. & Taillefer, S. (1997). *Somatoform disorders.* In S. M. Turner, & M. Hersen (Eds.), *Adult psychopathology and diagnosis* (3d Ed.). New York: John Wiley & Sons, Inc.

Lake, F. (1987). *Clinical Theology.* New York: Crossroad.

Lake, F. (1981). *Tight Corners in Pastoral Counselling.* London: Darton, Longman and Todd.

Lang, P. J. (1984). *The cognitive psychophysiology of emotion: Fear and anxiety.* In A. J. Tuma & J. D. Maser (Ed.), *Anxiety and anxiety disorders* (pp. 130–170). Hilldale, NJ: Erlbaum.

LeDoux, J. (1993). Emotional memory systems in the brain. *Behavioral and Brain Research,* 58, 24–39.

Leventhal, H. (1984). *A perceptual-motor theory of emotion.* In L. Berkowitz (Ed.), *Advances in experimental socialpsychology* (pp. 117–182). New York: Academic.

Leventhal, H., & Tomarken, R. (1986). *Emotion: Today's problems. Annual Review of Psychology,* 37, 565–610.

Levi, L. (1974). *Psychosocial stress and disease: A conceptual model.* In E. K. Gunderson & R. H. Rahe (Eds.), *Life stress and illness.* Springfield, IL: Charles C. Thomas.

Mayou, R., Bass, C., & Sharpe, M. (1995). *Overview of epidemiology, classification, and etiology.* In R. Mayou, C. Bass & M. Sharpe (Eds.), *Treatment of functional somatic symptoms* (pp. 42–65). Oxford: Oxford University Press.

Miranda, J., Perez-Stable, E., Munoz, R., Hargreaves, W., & Henke, C. (1991). *Somatization, psychiatric disorder, and stress in utilization of ambulatory medical services. Health Psychology,* 10, 46–51.

Nesse, R. M., & Williams, G. C. (1994). *Why we get sick. – The new science of Darwinian Medicine.* New York: Vintage Books.

Reid, W. H., Balis, G. U. & Sutton, B. J. (1997). *The treatment of psychiatric disorders* (3rd ed.). Bristol, PA: Brunner/Mazel, Inc.

Riedlinger, T., & Riedlinger, J. (1986). *Taking birth trauma seriously. Medical Hypotheses, 19,* 15–25.

Schore, A. N. (1994). *Affect regulation and the origin of the self. The neurobiology of emotional development.* Hillsdale, New Jersey: Lawrence Erlbaum Associates.

Terr, L. C. (1988). *What happens to early memories of trauma? Journal of the American Academy of Child and Adolescent Psychiatry,* 1, 96–104.

Thayer, R. E. (1989). *The biopsychology of mood and arousal.* New York: Oxford University Press.

van der Kolk, B. A. (1994). *The body keeps the score: Memory and the evolving psychobiology of posttraumatic stress. Harvard Review of Psychiatry,*](5), 253–265.

van der Kolk, B. A. (1989). *The compulsion to repeat the trauma: Re-enactment, re-victimization and masochism. Psychiatric Clinics of North America.* June, vol. 12, 389–411.

Journal of Prenatal and Perinatal Psychology and Health, 13(3–4), Spring/Summer 1999

The Importance of Prenatal Sound and Music

Giselle E. Whitwell, R.M.T.

INTRODUCTION

Music has profoundly affected human beings physically, mentally, emotionally and spiritually invirtually every culture throughout history. Yet only in this century has music begun to attract scientific attention. The research at the University of California at Irvine has provided some information about the effect of Mozart on the spatial and mathematical intelligence of children. Recently, an article in the Los Angeles Times (11/9/98) reported neurobiological research which indicates that "undeniably, there is a biology of music." Music is destined to play a more active role in the future of medicine. The following ideas illustrate how music affects our early development.

The importance of prenatal music was born in my own awareness over twenty years ago when I was expecting my youngest son. The doctor thought it would be dangerous for me to participate in something very active because the baby was was due that week, and since he was a second child stastically might arrive early, if not on time. Through my communication with the baby telepathically and his subsequent delay in arrival, I was able to attend a music conference that was very important to me. My son was born the day after I attended this stimulating week of singing and gentle movement.

Already at that time I observed that lullabies were relegated to the past. Young mothers no longer knew this folk song tradition. Michel Odent, M.D., believes that women have a profound need to sing to

Giselle Whitwell is a practicing prenatal music therapist in the Los Angeles area who has been a music educator for almost 20 years. For the last seven years, she has given lectures and workshops on prenatal music in the United States, Asia, and Europe. Please contact her at Winds, P.O. Box 280513, Northridge, CA 91328 or send email to <pre_natalmusic@yahoo.com>.

their babies but that the medicalization of birth has upset this process. In the past, women all over the world have sung lullabies to their babies. These were very important because as we now know the fetus is having first language lessons in the womb. The inflections of the mother tongue are conveyed not only through speech but most importantly through song. The singing voice has a richer frequency range than speech. In fact, studies in other disciplines such as linguistics and musicology (e.g., David Whitwell, 1993) point out that there was a time when speech was song and therefore singing is the older of the two. Babies born to deaf mothers miss these important first lessons in language development. French pioneer Dr. Alfred Tomatis mentions being intrigued by the fact that song birds hatched by silent foster mothers can't sing. What the baby learns in utero are the intonational patterns of sound and the frequencies of a language in his/her particular culture. Frequency is the level of pitch measured in Hertz (Hz.) This range varies between 16 to 20,000 Hz. There is very little distortion of the mother's voice as heard by the fetus whereas other external voices sound more muffled, especially in the higher frequencies. According to Rubel (1984), the fetus is responsive first to lower frequencies and then to higher ones.

Verny and others have noted that babies have a preference for stories, rhymes, and poems first heard in the womb. When the mother reads out loud, the sound is received by her baby in part via bone conduction. Dr. Henry Truby, Emeritus Professor of Pediatrics and Linguistics at the University of Miami, points out that after the sixth month, the fetus moves in rhythm to the mother's speech and that spectrographs of the first cry of an abortus at 28 weeks could be matched with his mother's. The elements of music, namely tonal pitch, timbre, intensity and rhythm, are also elements used in speaking a language. For this reason, music prepares the ear, body and brain to listen to, integrate and produce language sounds. Music can thus be considered a pre-linguistic language which is nourishing and stimulating to the whole human being, affecting body, emotions, intellect, and developing an internal sense of beauty, sustaining and awakening the qualities in us that are wordless and otherwise inexpressible.

The research of Polverini-Rey (1992) seems to indicate that prenates exposed to lullabies in utero were calmed by the stimulus. The famous British violinist Yehudi Menuhin believes that his own musical talent was partly due to the fact that his parents were always singing and playing music before he was born.

THE SOUND ENVIRONMENT OF THE WOMB

The sound environment of the womb is very rich. There are various interpretations as to the noise level, ranging between 30 to 96 dB. (decibel being a measure of sound intensity or loudness). A whisper can register 30 dB., a normal conversation is about 60 dB. and rush hour traffic can average about 70 dB. On the other hand, shouted conversations and motorcycles reach about 100 dB. Rock music has been measured as 115 dB. and the pain threshold begins at 125 dB. Yet, recent research with hydrophones have revealed that the womb is a "relatively quiet place" (Deliege and Sloboda, 1996), something comparable to what we experience in our environment between 50 and 60 dB.

Uterine sounds form a "sound carpet" over which the mother's voice in particular appears very distinct and which the prenate gives special attention because it is so different from its own amniotic environment. These sounds are of major importance because they establishes the first patterns of communication and bonding. Some researchers have discovered that newborns become calmer and more self-regulated when exposed to intrauterine sound (Murooka, et al., 1976; DeCasper, 1983; Rossner, 1979). The soothing sounds of the ocean and water are probably reminiscent of the fluid environment in which we began life. Tomatis suggests that the maternal heart beat, respiration and intestinal gurgling, all form the source for our collective attraction to the sound of surf and may have to do with our inborn sense of rhythm. Prenatal sounds form an important developmental component in prenatal life because they provide a foundation for later learning and behavior. With fetal sound stimulation the brain functions at a higher level of organization.

The ear first appears in the third week of gestation and it becomes functional by the 16th week. The fetus begins active listening by the 24th week. We know from ultrasound observations that the fetus hears and responds to a sound pulse starting about 16 weeks of age (Shahidullah & Hepper, 1992), even before the ear construction is complete. The cochlear structures of the ear appear to function by the 20th week and mature synapses have been found between the 24th and 28th weeks (Pujol, et al., 1991). For this reason most formal programs of prenatal stimulation are usually designed to begin during the third trimester. The sense of hearing is probably the most developed of all the senses before birth.

Four-month-old fetuses can respond in very specific ways to sound; if exposed to loud music their heart beat will accelerate. A Japanese study of pregnant women living near the Osaka airport had smaller babies and an inflated incidence of prematurity—arguably related to the environment of incessant loud noise. Chronic noise can also be associated with birth defects (Szmeja, et al., 1979). I recently received a report from a mother who was in her seventh month of pregnancy when she visited the zoo. In the lion's enclosure, the animals were in process of being fed. The roar of one lion would set off another lion and the sound was so intense she had to leave the scene as the fetus reacted with a strong kick and left her feeling ill. Many years later, when the child was seven years of age, it was found that he had a hearing deficiency in the lower-middle range. This child also reacts with fear when viewing TV programs of lions and related animals. There are numerous reports about mothers having to leave war movies and concerts because the auditory stimulus caused the fetus to become hyperactive.

Alfred Tomatis notes that the ear is "the Rome of the body" because almost all cranial nerves lead to it and therefore it is considered our most primary sense organ. Embryonically, according to him, the skin is differentiated ear, and we listen with our whole body.

In order to better understand the role of music in its elements of rhythm and melody, we must briefly clarify the two parts of the inner ear. These are the vestibular system and the cochlea. The vestibular system controls balance and body movements, including the integration of movements which make up the rhythm of music—making the vestibular system the more archaic. And according to Paul Madaule (1984) "it is in fact because of the vestibular system that music seems to have an impact on the body." At around four to six weeks gestational age the vestibular and the cochlear systems become differentiated, at seven the auditory ossicles start to grow, and at four months the ear of the fetus is already adult-like in shape and size. The cochlear system enables the transformation of acoustic vibrations into nervous influx, thus allowing the perception of melodies which carry higher frequencies. Knowing this, one can have a better understanding of the intimate relationship and unity of rhythm and melody. George Gershwin expressed this nicely: "Music sets up a certain vibration which unquestionably results in a physical reaction." With this in mind, we should choose for early music stimulation melodies and rhythms that are simple.

Tomatis has a unique view of the function of the human ear going beyond what is traditionally assumed. He regards it as neither an instrument solely for hearing and listening, nor an organ for the maintenance of equilibrium and verticality. For him the ear is primarily a generator of energy for the brain, intended to give a cortical charge which is then distributed throughout the body "with the view to toning up the whole system and imparting greater dynamism to the human being" (Gilmor and Madaule, 1984, p. 6). Hence the importance of right sound stimulation which will lead to vocal expression, listening, and thinking. Sound, music and human development are intricately interwoven.

Clearly, the vestibular system progresses rapidly as seen by the active movement of the fetus in utero. As early as the first trimester, regular exercise patterns have been observed with ultra-sound: rolling, flexing, turning, etc. (Van Dongen & Goudie, 1980). The movements appear as graceful somersaults, flexing of the back and neck, turning the head, waving arms, kicking legs—all self initiated and expressive in nature. When the baby moves in utero, the heartbeat accelerates. DeMause (1982) summarizes reactions of the second trimester as follows: "The fetus now floats peacefully, kicks, turns, sighs, grabs its umbilicus, gets excited at sudden noises, calms down when the mother talks quietly, and gets rocked back to sleep as she walks about."

The fetal heart is fully developed by the second trimester and its pulse rate oscillates between 120 to 160 beats per minute. Some think the distinctive rhythm of the mother's heart beat in utero is the basis and our attraction to drumming, rock rhythms, and the African tribal beat. Salk (1960), Murooka (1976), and De Casper (1983) provided evidence that newborns learned and remembered their mother's heart beat in utero. Ashley Montagu (1962) suggested that the universal appeal of music and the soothing effect of rhythmical sounds may be related to the feeling of well being assumed to exist in utero in relation to the mother's heartbeat. Salk (1960) showed that newborns in hospitals listening to heartbeat sounds gained weight at a faster rate. Likewise, breathing was deeper and more regular among these babies. According to W. Ernest Freud "rhythm itself provides a most reassuring 'cradle' because of its promise of repetition and continuity."

SOUND AND LEARNING IN UTERO

The powerful connection between sound/music and prenatal memory/learning have been revealed in formal experiments, parental observations, clinical records, and first person reports. Chamberlain (1998) using Howard Gardner's concept of multiple intelligences, has presented evidence for musical intelligence before birth. Peter Hepper

(1991) discovered that prenates exposed to TV soap opera music during pregnancy responded with focused and rapt attention to this music after birth—evidence of long-term memory. On hearing the music after birth, these newborns had a significant decrease in heart rate and movements, and shifted into a more alert state. Likewise, Shetler (1989) reported that 33% of fetal subjects in his study demonstrated contrasting reactions to tempo variations between faster and slower selections of music. This may be the earliest and most primitive musical response in utero.

The pioneering New Zealand fetologist, William Liley, found that from at least 25 weeks on, the unborn child would jump in rhythm with the timpanist's contribution to an orchestral performance. The research of Michele Clements (1977) in a London maternity hospital found that four to five month fetuses were soothed by Vivaldi and Mozart but disturbed by loud passages of Beethoven, Brahms and Rock. Newborns have shown a preference for a melody their mother sang in utero rather than a new song sung by their mother (Satt, 1987). Babies during the third trimester in utero respond to vibro-acoustic as well as air-coupled acoustic sounds, indicative of functional hearing. A study by Gelman, et al. (1982) determined that a 2000 Hz. stimulus elicited a significant increase in fetal movements, a finding which supported the earlier study by Johnsson, et al. (1964). From 26 weeks to term, fetuses have shown fetal heart accelerations in response to vibroacoustic stimuli. Consistent startle responses to vibroacoustic stimuli were also recorded during this period of development. Behavioral reactions included arm movements, leg extensions, and head aversions (Birnholz and Benacerraf, 1983). Yawning activity was observed after the conclusion of stimuli. Research by Luz, et al. (1980 and 1985) has found that the normal fetus responds to external acoustic stimulation during labor in childbirth. These included startle responses to the onset of a brief stimulus.

New evidence of cognitive development in the prenatal era is presented by William Sallenbach (1998) who made in-depth and systematic observations of his own daughter's behavior from weeks 32 to 34 in utero. Until recently, most research on early learning processes has been in the area of habituation (Querleu, et al., 1981), conditioning (Van de Carr, 1988) or imprinting sequences (Salk, 1962). However, Sallenbach observed that in the last trimester of pregnancy, the prenate's learning state shows movement from abstraction and generalization to one of increased specificity and differentiation. During a bonding session using music, the prenate was observed moving her hands gently. In a special musical arrangement, where dissonance was included, the subject's reactions were more rhythmic with rolling movements. Similarly, in prenatal music classes, Sister Lorna Zemke has found that the fetus will respond rhythmically to rhythms tapped on the mother's belly.

From what research is telling us, we may presume that prenates would prefer to hear lullabies sung by their mothers, or selected slow passages of Baroque music such as Vivaldi, Telemann, and Handel which have a tempo resembling our own heart beat at rest. Recent research has shown that four month old infants demonstrate an innate preference for music that is consonant rather than dissonant (Zentner and Kagan, 1998). However, this allows great latitude in the selection of music which babies and their mothers might like to hear. Our ultimate objective, of course is to help create not a musical genius but a person well integrated in his physical, emotional, intellectual and spiritual self.

REFERENCES

Campbell, Don. (1997). The Mozart Effect, New York: Avon Books.

Chamberlain, David B. (1994). The sentient prenate: What every parent should know. *Pre- and Perinatal Psychology Journal,* 9(1), 9–31.

Chamberlain, David B. (1998). Prenatal receptivity and intelligence. *Journal of Prenatal and Perinatal Psychology and Health,* 12(3 and 4), 95–117.

Clements, Michele (1977). Observations on certain aspects of neonatal behavior in response to auditory stimuli. Paper presented to the 5th Internat. Congress of Psychosomatic Obstetrics and Gynecology, Rome.

DeCasper, A. and Sigafoos. (1983). The intrauterine heartbeat: A potent reinforcer for newborns. *Infant Behavior and Development,* 6, 19–25.

DeCasper, A. and Spence. (1986). Prenatal maternal speech influences newborns' perception of speech sounds. *Infant Behavior and Development,* 9, 133–150.

Deliege, Irene and Sloboda, John (Eds.). (1996). Musical Beginnings, Oxford University Press.

Gilmor, Timothy M. and Madaule, Paul P. (1984). The Tomatis Anthology. Toronto: The Listening Centre.

Odent, Michel. (1984). Birth Reborn. New York: Pantheon Books.

Shahidullah, Sara and Hepper, Peter. (1992). Hearing in the fetus: Prenatal detection of deafness. *Int. J. Prenatal and Perinatal Studies,* 4(3 and 4), 235–240.

Shetler, Donald J. (1989). The inquiry into prenatal musical experience: A report of the Eastman Project 1980–1987. *Pre- and Peri-Natal Psychology Journal,* 3(3), 171–189.

Whitwell, David. (1993). Music As A Language: A New Philosophy Of Music Education. Northridge, CA: Winds.

Woodward, Sheila C. (1992). The Transmission Of Music Into The Human Uterus And The Response To Music Of The Human Fetus And Neonate (Doctoral Thesis, Dept. of Music Education, University of Cape Town, South Africa.

Zentner, Marcel R. and Kagan, Jerome. (1998). Infant's perception of consonance and dissonance in music. *Infant Behavior and Development,* 21(3), 483–492.

FOR STUDY IN GREATER DEPTH

Birnholz, J. C. and Benacerraf, B. B. (1983). The development of the human fetal hearing. *Science*, 222, 516–18.

DeCasper, A. J. and Sigafoos, A. D. (1983). The intrauterine heartbeat: A potent reinforcer for newborns. *Infant Behavior and Development*, 6, 19–25.

deMause, L. (1982). Foundations of psychohistory. New York: Creative Roots.

Gelman, S. R., Wood, S., Spellacy, W. N. and Abrams, R. M. (1982). Fetal movements in response to sound stimulation. *American J. of Obstetrics and Gynecology*, 143, 484–485.

Hepper, P. G. (1991). An examination of fetal learning before and after birth. *The Irish Journal of Psychology*, 12(2), 95–107.

Johansson, B., Wedenberg, E., and Westin, B. (1964). Measurement of tone response by the human fetus. A preliminary report. *Acta Otolaryngologica*, 57, 188–192.

Luz, N. P., Lima, C. P., Luz, D. H., & Feldens, V. L. (1980). Auditory evoked responses of the human fetus. I. Behavior during progress of labor. *Acta Obstetrica Gynecologica Scandinavica*, 59, 395–404.

Luz, N. P. (1985). Auditory evoked responses in the human fetus. II. Modifications observed during labor. *Acta Obstetrica Gynecologica Scandinavica*, 64, 213–22.

Montagu, A. (1962). Prenatal influences. Springfield, IL: Charles Thomas.

Murooka H., Koie Y., & Suda N. (1976). Analyse des sons intra-uterins et leurs effets tranquil-lisants sur le nouveau. *Journal of Gynecology and Obstetrics: Biologie de la Reproduction*, 5, 367–376.

Polverini-Rey, R. A. (1992). Intrauterine musical learning: the soothing effect on newborns of a lullaby learned prenatally. Dissertation Abstracts # 9233740.

Pujol, R., Lavigne-Rebillard, M., and Uziel, A. (1991). Development of the human cochlea. *Acta Otolaryngologica*, 482, 7–12.

Querleu, D., Renard, S., and Versyp, F. (1981). Les perceptions auditives du foetus humain. *Medecine et Hygiene*, 39, 2101–10.

Rosner, B. S., & Doherty, N. E. (1979). The response of neonates to intra-uterine sounds. *Developmental Medicine and Child Neurology*, 21, 723–729.

Salk, L. (1962). Mother's heartbeat as an imprinting stimulus. *Transactions of the New York Academy of Sciences, Series 2*, 4, 753–63.

Salk, L. (1960). The effects of the normal heartbeat sound on the behavior of newborn infant: implications for mental health. *World Mental Health*, 12, 1–8.

Sallenbach, W. B. (1998). Claira: A case study in prenatal learning. *Journal of Pre- and Perinatal Psychology and Health*, 12(3–4), 175–196.

Satt, B. J. (1984). An investigation into the acoustical induction of intra-uterine learning. Ph.D Dissertation, Californian School of Professional Psychology, Los Angeles.

Shetler, Donald J. (1989). The Inquiry Into Prenatal Musical Experience: A Report of the Eastman Project 1980–1987. *Pre- and Perinatal Psychology Journal*, 3(3), 171–189.

Szmeja, Z., Slomko, Z., Sikorski, K., and Sowinski, H. (1979) The risk of hearing impairment in children from mothers exposed to noise during pregnancy, *Int. Journal of Pediatric Otorhinolaryngology*, 1, 221–29.

Van de Carr, Kristen., Van de Carr, F. Rene., and Lehrer, Marc. (1988). Effects of a prenatal intervention program. In P. Fedor-Freybergh and Vogel, M.L.V., (Eds.), Prenatal and perinatal psychology and medicine: Encounter with the unborn (pp. 489–495). London: Parthenon Publishing.

Van Dongen, L. G. R. and Goudie, E. G. (1980). Fetal movements in the first trimester of pregnancy. *British Journal of Obstetrics and Gynecology*, 87, 191–193.

Journal of Prenatal and Perinatal Psychology and Health, 13(3–4), Spring/Summer 1999

Before I Am, We Are

Mac Freeman, Ph.D.

It is only a few years since I, a psychologically trained and educationally active father of four came to realize that a baby in its mother's womb is NOT like a little potato, swelling up in the dark until the time comes to rise to the surface, to be cut off from its vine, washed and pruned, to await, in a few days, the opening of its eyes. I was not a backward father out of touch with "common knowledge"; rather, "common knowledge" was until recently out of touch with the facts of this amazing little creature that we call a human baby. From a single cell smaller than a pencil tip, in some 40 weeks there burgeons a self-launching "rocket ship" increasingly ready to monitor its many internal interlocking systems in preparation for the countdown, which normally the ship itself calls for when its internal communications network is ready to operate effectively during its traumatic transition, which we call its birth. Hardly a blind potato in the dark! "Common knowledge" still insists that a baby is born when it leaves its mother's body. Yet if we had not been raised to equate birth with the delivery and earlier had the facts now available on the development of this human offspring, we might well have delayed a baby's actual birthday until a half year or so after the day of delivery. By that time the infant would be self-propelling, self-feeding, and able to travel with its mother like many other newborn mammals.

It is even more recently that another realisation has come into my head full of "common knowledge". A human baby does not start off as an I but as a part of We. I expect that most mothers on hearing me say that would exclaim, "Well, of course! Any mother knows that!" There are cultural subgroups in which persons start off as We and also end up still as We. But in our North American white, male-dominant culture the emphasis has increasingly centered on I, first and

Mac Freeman is Professor Emeritus, Faculty of Education Queen's University, Kingston, Ontario, Canada.

last. Not on I and We, but on I and Me (SEE APENDIX). When I was a child, I learned as "common knowledge" that most persons are I-centred by nature. To be generously concerned for others is a morally good attitude to be developed, or instilled by societal pressure. A few years ago, I learned that the renowned researcher into the development of children, Jean Piaget, had derived an axiomatic conclusion confirming "common knowledge", that "the child's initial universe is entirely centered on his own body and action is an egocentrism as total as it is unconscious (for lack of consciousness of the self)." (Piaget and Inhelder, 1969, p. 13) But by that time, I as a father had observed some infants who seemed to be exceptions to Piaget's dictum, in that they could entice me and other adults around them to play with them in joyous interaction. Then I ran across some research findings confirming my sense that infants are quite capable of being part of We. Condon and Sander of Boston University made a remarkable discovery, which they published in 1974. Using microanalysis of high speed sound films of mothers speaking privately to their babies between 12 hours and 2 days after delivery they found that even at this early age, (and it may be as early as minutes after delivery), babies move in synchrony with their mother's voice, as do the mothers, thus executing a sort of dance. Specific body movements are linked with particular sounds, with such regularity that one can learn to predict just how a baby will move when its mother addresses any communication to that baby. A casual onlooker misses this subtle linkage, but the attentive mother does not; rather she is "turned on" by her baby's responses to her.

Commenting on this responsiveness between newborn and mother, Dr. T. Berry Brazelton, a leading neonatologist of Harvard and Boston, likened it to the "mating dance" of swans (Brazelton, 1976, p. 74). For further confirmation of the reality of We-oriented behaviour by infants, examine these observations by Brazelton, et al. published in 1975:

> We are convinced that in a "good" interaction, mother and baby synchronize with each other from the beginning and that pathways may be set up in intrauterine life, ready to be entrained, especially by the mother immediately after birth. Intrauterine experience with other maternal cues, such as auditory or kinesthetic, may well set the stage for enhancing the meaning of the synchronous rhythms. Rhythmic interaction seems to be basic to human affect. (Brazelton, 1975, p.148)

It seems that before I am, We are, in primal ways.

Yet we all know about "terrible two's" and about children "wanting their own way" to the extent of having a temper tantrum in the supermarket. We remember our own childhood yearnings to become competent as *I* and to be validated by significant others. Can someone now make sense for us of a developmental journey from a primal propensity for *We* through the terrible two's and later, through adolescent rebellion focused entirely on *I* to a mature propensity for We and I? As I have pondered the complex interweavings of We and I, what I have come to call "the dynamics of We and Me", I have been assisted by the metaphor of "duet". In a bona fide duet there are two developing centers of self-expression, two I's, but each also is learning to be attuned to their We to achieve the duet interaction. Accordingly, this duet is made possible by both "duet soloing" and "attunement", both being competencies to be developed but also naturally wired into us from birth. Duet soloing is familiar to anyone who has watched a superb doubles match in tennis, or Olympic skating pairs as they interact in their precise dance, or "No. 99"—Wayne Gretsky, as he combines his dazzling individual prowess with his equally dazzling assistance to his hockey teammates. For such duet soloing, a willingness to listen is a prerequisite combined with a capacity for empathy with the energy, the pacing, and even the mood of the duet partner.

Exquisite self-control must be learned to match the moves of the partner, while at the same time expressing one's solo artistry. The attunement competency is like having an ear for resonance, for "picking up the vibes" and adapting to them. But it is even more complex because each would-be member of the duo must first know what the other is doing. This coming-to-know process entails a "decoding". Each has to read new signals and make sense of them to collaborate appropriately. A duet is not always balanced like a seesaw: one partner may be more developed than the other. Nevertheless, attunement is possible so that old and young, senior and junior, veteran and amateur, can enter into duet. It requires a patient effort by the more advanced partner, who is able to be more responsive to the duet possibility, not to remain in that imbalance but to foster the development toward balance. A mother and infant duet starts off imbalanced.

How early does their duet start? I was pondering that pivotal question some years ago when another surprising thought came into my head to jar my "common knowledge", and this one, like the others, has by now become insistent. I had been listening to a Capitol recording called *Lullaby from the Womb,* made by a Japanese obstetrician, Dr. Hajime Murooka. (This recording has recently been re-issued on cassette.) On one side I had heard recorded the pumping sound of the maternal hydraulic system as picked up by a small microphone placed in the uterus beside the head of an eight month fetus. The pulsating "body beat" is deep and "whooshy", its frequency that of the pregnant mother's heartbeat, around 90 beats per minute. On the reverse side are several beloved classical music selections, each with a fundamental rhythm close to that of the maternal heartbeat. Bach's "Air on the G String", on the second band, led me to the notion that my fondness for that piece of music could be related to remembering the rhythm I had once heard or felt in my mother's womb. Dr. Murooka reports on the record jacket that "of the 403 sobbing babies who listened to the tape, every single one stopped crying, with 161 infants dozing off to sleep in an average of 41 seconds".

The thought of a possible connection between music we love and our mother's heartbeat excited me and it raised other conjectures, about aboriginal drumming, about the big lush beat in many country and western favourites, and the too-fast-for-me beat in much contemporary pop music. I thought of comments made by war veterans concerning Scottish pipe bands. They insisted that "you could march all day to their beat and not get tired". But then came a startling new thought, triggered by hearing the last selection on side 2 of Murooka's *Lullaby,* — "Panorama" from *The Sleeping Beauty* by Tchaikovsky. This music has the same hydraulic pulsation, but I suddenly heard a second beat, faster and higher-pitched. . . . Like the fetal heartbeat? The thought stunned me! Dare I speculate that Tchaikovsky so composed that music because he remembered a *rhythmic duet* in his mother's womb? Could it be true that we are drawn to it as a favorite because we too find the duet to be familiar? I was told, on inquiring, that the heart of a prenate starts beating the 25th day after conception, about 180 times per minute and gradually slows down to 120 by delivery time: the maternal frequency starts around 80 beats per minute, and gradually increases to 95 or 100. Thus the ratio of the two frequencies varies considerably, but may average about 2:1. Then my speculation *might* not be wild?

I dared to set my hearing to pick up rhythmic duets in other favorite music, and lo, they are there in abundance! I began to watch the clapping hands and tapping toes of musical performers and their audience; I talked to a professional drummer from a Forties big band; I studied fingers strumming guitar strings; I heard in a new way what may be the most beloved of all classical pieces—Pachelbel's *Canon,* I was soothed deeply by Mozart's twenty-first Piano Concerto, the second movement, which is the familiar "Elvira Madigan" music, I was "grabbed", like most other listeners, by an amazing electronic rendition of *Oxygène* by Jean Michel Jarre. And I "found" what has become my favorite country and western song—*Willow in the Wind* as sung by Kathy Mattea. A rhythmic duet was manifest in all of them!

I knew that Native peoples sometimes speak of the drum as being the "heartbeat" of Mother Earth. Accordingly, when the opportunity came for me to watch Native men around one big drum, I was all eyes and ears. But when the drumming began I was puzzled—they were beating too fast for a usual maternal frequency, about twice too fast ...? Then I saw a Native woman standing beside them, moving to every second beat! I explored music made by Québec Inuit people, expecting to hear a characteristic drumbeat, but instead I heard remarkable throat singing by three women at a concert: their *Song of a Tree* and *Song of the River* and other songs pulsated just like the recorded mother's hydraulic system. I was not able to be present to watch for a twice-as-fast second frequency in the movement of bodies in their audience, but I am confident it was there somewhere. A student returning from Nepal reported seeing folk-dancing each evening by the people of an isolated mountain village, the women in one circle and the men in another concentric circle, dancing to two frequencies matching those of the mother and fetus!

By now I was intuiting a memory of two beats interacting, because, to put it in fun terms, each of us was gestated within a jam session featuring two drummers for 24 hours a day for about 36 weeks. The fetal child is one of the drummers, i.e., its pulsating system, and the mother is the other, through her pulsating womb. But what about persons who are not musically inclined? Would they have a corresponding fascination for two interacting beats? So I began to ask persons in every audience available whether they had an inclination to avoid stepping on the cracks in the sidewalk. (As one walks along, one's feet tap out one frequency, and the sidewalk cracks passing underneath mark out another, which is about half as fast.) Sure enough, there would be a ripple of amusement in every audience as many admitted their fascination with how these two frequencies relate to each other. Then I would ask how many were drawn in by the two windshield wipers on buses to see whether they would ever get in step. This question drew much laughter every time. It seems that windshield wiper watching on buses is almost an obsession! Why?! Two interacting frequencies again!

Had I found sufficient evidence to justify a hypothesis that you and I were a duo with our mother from almost the beginning of our development? I wanted more. So, if there are two hearts beating in a 1: 2 ratio and the mother's beat speeds up, does the fetal beat also speed up? Yes. How quickly does it respond to the change? I still do not know enough about this, but I began to play with the possibility that with some time lag between maternal heartbeat and fetal heart adjustment, there would be for the fetus the feeling of rhythmic syncopation. This rhythm would happen over and over again. Who knows how this subtle shift could be registered in a prenate's memory, but surely it is interesting in this connection that many of us really like Dixieland music which is packed full of rhythmic syncopation. Listen to the Preservation Hall jazz band playing Blues and be "torn apart" by the shifting frequencies. The noteworthy thing is, we LIKE it, it feels "right" even though formally, it is "wrong". Did J. S. Bach also "know" this when he wrote his six Brandenburg Concertos?

I suppose the supreme test of my hunch would come in the case of twins, where three "drummers", not just two, would be interacting. I recall vividly a night in Naramata Centre, British Columbia, when I was speaking to an audience about this duet theory: at the end of my talk a middle-aged woman stood before me, tears streaming down her cheeks as she said, "All my life I have loved music with three beats. I have never understood why until tonight—I am a twin whose brother died at birth."

About this same time I received a remarkable confirmation of the primal duo from two parents, both Special Education teachers. In their account of the gestation of their two children, a girl then two and a boy, age one. During each pregnancy both mother and father had sought to send repeated messages in to their babies. The mother beamed in love as she read aloud in their quiet home each afternoon. The father on arriving home from school each day, said "Yoo Hoo, I'm home" from just outside the mother's abdomen. From 25 weeks on, in both pregnancies, an astonishing thing happened: every day, as the father said his words on one side, a bulge appeared there; when the father shifted his voice to the other side, the bulge went over there. Back and forth from side to side, every day for the 15 remaining weeks, in both pregnancies, father and fetus played tag! The very close bonding of the newborns with both parents was dramatically manifest and has strongly continued in the years since.

I am now persuaded that for human beings, the first natural learning habitat is in duet. That the interplay of two beats draws us is undeniable, but I think this is only an indication of our profound readiness for interactive, interdependent, "duocentered" development almost from the beginning. It is no fluke that babies right after delivery will imitate the facial expression of the adult nearest them (Meltzoff and Moore at the University of Washington, reported by Schiefelbein, 1986, p. 39). It is no one-in-a-million happening that newborns move in compelling ways so as to "capture" their caregivers. (Brazelton, 1985, xi) It is no chance variation that an infant begins to learn its mother tongue through interaction with its primary caregiver and even earlier, while in the womb!

As a duet/soloist in the making, a human infant comes equipped with a remarkably sensitive attunement capacity comprised at least of an aptitude for decoding the strange signalling of its primal duet partner plus an aptitude for adapting its own signalling for the sake of resonance. I have not yet worked through how the decoding and adapting for resonance flow into the complex mental powers of the burgeoning child. I surmise that where the sensitive receptiveness of the infant is overtaxed, blocking/filtering out can occur. Not that one bad day will ruin a life, for a baby is very resilient and there is some built-in protection against overload.

Of course, if a mother is psychologically unbalanced and thus unavailable for consistent, positive duet learning, then the fetal child must learn *not* to reach out for a duet partner. Duetting itself might prove so painfully unpredictable that it would be filtered out as an option. Research has shown that newborn infants of sighted mothers turn first to the mother's eyes for a response, while infants of blind mothers, having tried the eyes, turn to mother's hands. Infants of weakly sighted mothers waffle between eyes and hands. Maybe similarly, an infant with a psychotic mother seeks in her eyes, her hands and in all else about her, consistent signals to decode for mutual resonating, but in vain, so gives up on duetting. How would such duet deprivation affect the infant's subsequent interactions? Might he/she come to declare with Piaget that all human infants are egocentric, because he/she had to be so, to survive at all? Might the meaning-making following upon that early loss and the resulting decoding bias be diverted away from affirming human interdependence and move instead toward a declaration of independence, starting in infancy and peaking in adulthood?

In his 1990 book, *Iron John, a Book About Men,* Robert Bly declared:

> When we are tiny we have the feeling we are God. Our kingly life in the womb pointed to some such possibility, and if anyone, once we are out, tries to tell us we are not God, we don't hear it. (p. 33)

I am curious what led Bly to that biased generalization. In the case of Piaget's generalization about infant egocentrism, he himself has said somewhere in his writings that his mother was psychotic. One must be wary of drawing hasty conclusions, but the omission of any reference to the mother's personal contribution to her children, from Piaget's summative work, *The Psychology of the Child* (1969), tempts one to do so. The mother is represented in that book only by "the nipple", her caregiving is reduced to nothing more than responding to the "the sucking reflex". (p. 7)

A great deal of study is needed to refine an understanding of infant duocentric development, but already, the possible implications and ramifications are far-reaching. How many North American school-children today are duet-damaged or worse, duet-deprived? One hears reports of increasing student hypertension and restlessness to the point of unmanageability. Are these children behaving just like fish out of water, because they have been deprived in infancy of their water of duetting? Were their parents unable to continue in duet with them after delivery because they themselves had been duet-damaged earlier and accordingly, carried their own decoding bias against resonant re-lating? (Note the generational spiralling potential.) Were those par-ents once among those infants for whom hospital procedures, at that time, were disruptive of mother-newborn relating? Had their school teachers along the way been similarly duet-damaged, so that their ways of managing children did not offer much by way of duet recovery, and thereby exacerbated the filtered "independence" of these stu-dents? (Some might call it "armoured aloneness".) Of course, there were other factors to be considered in the socio-cultural flow, like the emergence of the nuclear family to be an emotional hothouse, and the increasing occurrence of single parent families, where too much can be expected for too long of too few.

One must not fall into single factor causation, but one is tempted to link much of the malaise in our society today, including the batter-ing, the addictions, and under it all, the anxious individualism, to the fundamental flaw of duet damage. If it be true that duetting is the water in which human fish are made to swim (first), then we must consider the disquieting possibility that we are witnessing now the frantic struggles to survive of a host of fish-persons out of water.

In a very recent conversation, another new thought has come: each time there is a breakdown of mother-infant duet, the mother also is duet-damaged or deprived. During pregnancy her being has antici-pated relating closely with her baby. Forces deeper than her conscious choice have predisposed her for duetting. But if negative procedures and attitudes jeopardize the sensitive beginning of the duo and in-stead of the mother/child "duetting dance" flowing, it becomes a du-tiful "forced march", the loss to the mother could also be enormous. She may bounce back. Like a baby, the mother also can be very resil-ient. But she may not recover. How many women are carrying the resulting loss?

CONCLUSION

At the risk of being superficial in my brief comments, let me nevertheless relate these conclusions about our primal duettedness and the duet damage rampant in North American society to several current themes and movements.

There is much said now about "co-dependence". Melody Beattie's 1987 best-seller by that name had this definition on the cover:

"Codependent, a person who has let someone else's behavior affect him or her and is obsessed with controlling other people's behavior."

Anne Wilson Schaef, in her 1987 best-seller, *When Society Becomes an Addict,* wrote of the addictive relationship as the basic relationship within North American culture:

> It is a "cling-clung" relationship. Both persons involved are convinced that they cannot exist without it. They see themselves as two half-persons who must stick together to make a whole. They arrive at decisions in tandem. They practically synchronize their breathing. We are taught from an early age to call the addictive relationship by another name: true love. True love is when two people are incapable of functioning or even surviving without each other. We are also taught from an early age that the way to attain "security" is by establishing such a mutual dependency. (p. 26)

Is this a sort of inverse duetting, fostered by duet damage in infants who struggle into cling-clung adulthood, there to lock into "true love" as better than no relating at all?

A key element in the socio-cultural analysis provided by Schaef is dependency:

> a state in which you assume that someone or something outside of you will take care of you because you cannot take care of yourself. Dependent persons rely on others to meet their emotional, psychological, intellectual, and spiritual needs. (p. 72)

Recovery from dependency comes with the realization that one can rely on oneself and take care of oneself while also staying close to others. "True intimacy requires us to be . . . whole in and of ourselves. . . ." (p.73) If one brings to the same situation the metaphor of duet, so that one values interdependence between duet soloists, the analysis could turn out differently.

In Schaef's incisive analysis of the "Addictive System" in our society, she wrote:

> In the Addictive System, *the self is central.* Everyone and everything must go through, be related to, and be defined by the self as perceived by the self.
> The Addictive system . . . really believes that is is possible to be God as defined

by that system. In holding this belief, it also assumes that it has the right to define everything, which is the epitome of self-centeredness. (pp. 40–41)

I think it is confusing to equate being dependent and being in dependency. Also, I wonder if one can really be whole in and of oneself. Terry Kellogg in his 1990 book, *Broken Toys, Broken Dreams,* parallelled what I am thinking in reaction to the currently popular downgrading of dependent behavior:

Independents are led to believe they were always on their own: a hard baby to hold, always squiggling, did things their own way, played alone, etc. The independent buys the myth of their separateness and differentness without realizing they became independent, not because of who or what they are, but because there was no one around for them to depend on. (p. 9)

Kellogg has provided a less confusing word than dependency—"enmeshment"—"defining ourselves through others, suffering for and because of others . . . when we can't tell where we stop and others begin . . . arrested individuation in childhood." (p. 10) He wants us instead to have both intimacy and detachment in relating: "detachment means we still care and feel but are no longer controlled" (p. 11). But surely detachment is not a good word to link with caring and feeling. The duet metaphor would serve well here.

John Bradshaw in his analysis on the wounded child says much but not all that is congruent with my conclusions. In his his 1990 book, *Homecoming,* he indicates that:

We first see the world through the eyes of a little child, and that inner world remains with us throughout our lives. . . . If our vulnerable child was hurt or abandoned, shamed or neglected, that child's pain, grief, and anger live on within us. I believe that this neglected, wounded inner child of the past is the major source of human misery.
    Yes.
Reclaiming your inner child involves going back through your developmental stages and finishing your unfinished business.
    Probably.
With you as his nurturing and protective parent, your wounded inner child can begin the process of healing. You will connect with a fresh vision of your child, enriched by your years of adult experience. This is your true homecoming. It is a discovery of your essence, your deepest, unique self.
    No.

I am persuaded, contrary to John Bradshaw, that in the dynamics of We and Me, there is no shortcut back to We *through* Me. How could a duet-damaged or deprived child *cum* adult rise up to offer duet-healing to oneself? Although Bradshaw here and there pointed his readers beyond self-healing to a healing relationship with a "Higher Power", and though he also acknowledged that "a child's healthy

growth depends on someone loving and accepting him unconditional-
ly", (p. 39), he also declared on the very next page that "in reclaiming
and championing your wounded inner child, you give him the positive
unconditional acceptance that he craves." (p. 40) It would be deeply
regrettable if Bradshaw's zealous effort, which is urgently needed in
this sick society, is thus flawed.

Another healing thrust is coming from "Re-evaluation Counselling",
which was launched by Harvey Jackins in the 1960's and by now has
spread to many countries. One of its fundamental affirmations is that
humans are naturally given to mutual co-operation and enjoyable
communication with each other (Jackins, 1978, p. 27). In the co-coun-
selling that participants offer to each other in dyads, the basic activity
is co-listening so as to take turns releasing the stress blocking the
effective living of each partner. This is totally compatible with my
conclusions about our essential duettedness.

At the Stone Centre in Wellesley College, Massachusetts, there is
work in progress on "relational theory". A paper presented at a Stone
Centre Colloquium in November, 1990, by Stephen J. Bergman, M.D.,
Ph.D., on "Men's Psychological Development: A Relational Perspective" has been summarised as follows:

> Current theories of male psychological development emphasise the primary im-
> portance of the "self" and fail to describe the whole of men's experience in rela-
> tionship. Men as well as women are motivated by a primary desire for connection,
> and it is less accurate and useful to think of "self" than "self-in-relation" as a
> process. As with women, the sources of men's misery are in disconnections, vio-
> lations, and in dominances, and in participating in relationships which are not
> mutually empowering. . . . (Bergman, 1991, p. 1)

This surely was an enlightening paper. The duet metaphor and duocentric development theory could be a constructive complement.

Another complementary contribution has been provided by Riane
Eisler's research and labors pertaining to partnership. In her study of
major currents in human history as reported in her 1987 book, *The
Chalice and the Blade,* she found running throughout, two conflicting
paradigms, "partnership" and "dominator". Like Fritjof Capra in *The
Turning Point* (1982), and Thomas Berry in *The Dream of the Earth*
(1988), Eisler sees an urgent need for a paradigm shift if the human
species is to thrive or possibly to survive at all: Capra has called for
the recognition **now** of the essential interrelatedness and interdependence of all phenomena—in "the systems view of life". (p. 265) Berry
seeks the healing of the earth through a "mutually enhancing human
presence to the earth community" (p. 212): Eisler would foster a shift
from a dominator model of human relations to a partnership model

"in which social relations are primarily based on the principle of *linking* rather than ranking. . . ." (xvii) Unlike Capra and Berry, however, Eisler has hope that such a basic turning may be possible as a *returning,* in that some 5000 years ago, according to recent archeological research findings, there actually was an era of partnership which proved to be both workable and productive of human and earthly well-being.

Now if it be also true that we as human beings begin our personal development as duettable and thus *partnership-prone,* there is another good reason for that hope.

Before I am, We are. But what if on my developmental journey I was deprived of duet and alienated from attunement, so that without We, I now thrash about without integrity of spirit or integration of action, is there for me any way forward? This is surely an urgent question.

Maybe that way forward can begin by my being taken back to the time, early in gestation, before my primal duet dance was interrupted, to be "recalled" there by music carrying the duet rhythms that accompanied my very early thriving. I am prompted to suggest this primal duet recall approach by an experience I had with "Frank", an abandoned 14 year-old student in a residential school. He had been born out of wedlock to a mother who immediately turned him over to her parents to raise. Then she died, followed soon by her parents' deaths, leaving Frank utterly alone. He had survived somehow in foster settings, and at 14 was highly artistic, socially withdrawn, uncommunicative and suicidal. I met him when he, having overheard some rhythmic duet excerpts which I played from the record *Oxygène* by Jean Michel Jarre, came up to me to express his preference for "that breathing music". While I replayed the excerpts for him he put his ear right up to the speaker box to listen intently, and then he said, "That music makes me feel important."! After that, in the days following, he and I worked together on a building project in that school, and he was co-operative and enthusiastic, as if he had a new lease on life. So I wonder what would happen if teachers and principals were to build into the school curriculum "music for primal duet recall". It might be conveyed through invitational "dancercize" activity for students *and staff,* to open each school day. Or it might be built into the curriculum by individual teachers in ways still to be worked out. Parents too might be drawn into the exploration of "healing music in education". All of this remedial effort is urgently important because what fish out of water need *first* is not to be taught how to be fish, but to be brought back into the water.

Joanna Macy is an American "despair worker", becoming ever more widely known for her book *Despair and Power in the Nuclear Age.* In a 1989 conversation with her, recorded in Catherine Ingram's book *In the footsteps of Gandhi: Conversations with spiritual social activists,* there is this exchange:

> Ingram: Our entire media colludes in this hysteria of: "We're great, we're wonderful, let us wave the flag and pledge allegiance. We may have some problems but this is still the greatest country in the world, rah, rah.". . . . The house is burning on many levels, as you well know. And yet there are so many people still in denial about it. What is beneath this tremendous denial?
> Macy: I think it has to do with the notion of the self that our culture has conditioned us to believe through its emphasis on individualism. That view and the way it is conveyed puts a tremendous burden on a person in terms of holding himself together, in terms of competition, in terms of defendedness. . . .
> So what's drawing me more and more is to work directly on that notion of the self and provide people with experiences and illustrations that can help them shed that old notion of self. . . . they want to be invited to come home to the way of participation in this world, knowing that they are part of the web of life, which in our heart of hearts is what we want most. (pp. 164–65)

Can we hope that however frantically the fish out of water thrash about, what they really want, more than anything else, is the water of their life? From the 13th century poet, Rumi, this comment:

> I have a thirsty fish in me that can never find enough of what it is thirsty for! Show me the way to the Ocean! (trans. Coleman Barks)

My perisistent hunch is that the way to the Ocean lies through music.

REFERENCES

Barks, C. & Moyne, J. trs. (1988). *This longing — Poetry, teaching stories & selected letters of J. Rumi.* Threshold, Vt.

Beattie, M. (1987). *Codependence.* Hazelden.

Bergman, S. J. (1991) *Men's Psychological Development: A Relational Perspective,* Work in progress, No. 48. Wellesley, Mass. The Stone Center, Wellesley College.

Berry, T. (1988). *The dream of the earth.* San Francisco: Sierra Club Books.

Bly, R. (1990). *Iron John. A book about men.* New York: Addison-Wesley.

Bradshaw, J. (1990). *Homecoming. Reclaiming and championing your inner child.* New York: Bantam Books.

Brazelton, T. B. (1976). Comment, *Maternal-infant bonding.* Klaus, M. H. and Kennell, J. H., St. Louis: Mosby.

Brazelton, T. B. (1985). Introduction, *The biography of a baby,* M. Washburn Shinn, Reading, Mass.: Addison-Wesley.

Brazelton, T. B. et al. (1975). Early mother-infant reciprocity, *Parent-infant interaction.* Ciba Foundation Symposium 33 (new series). Amsterdam: Associated Scientific Publishers.

Capra, F. (1982). *The turning point: Science, society and the rising culture.* New York: Bantam Books.

Condon, W. S. and Sander, L. W. (1974). Neonate Movement is Synchronized with Adult Speech, *Science,* 183.

Eisler, R. (1987). *The chalice and the blade. Our history, our future.* San Francisco, Harper & Row.

Ingram, C. (1990). *In the footsteps of Ghandi: Conversations with spiritual social activists.* Berkeley, Cal.: Parallax Press.

Jackins, H. (1978). *The human side of human beings: The theory of re-evaluation counselling.* 2nd rev. ed. Seattle: Rational Island Publshers.

Jarre, J. M. (1977). *Oxygène.* Polydor.

Jordan, J. V., Kaplan, A. G., Miller, J. B., Stiver, I. P. and Surrey, J. L. (1991). *Women's growth in connection.* Writings from the Stone Center. New York: Guilford Press.

Kellogg, T. (1990). *Broken toys, broken dreams. Understanding and healing boundaries, co-dependence, compulsive behaviors, and family relationships.* Amherst, Mass: BRAT Publishing.

Murooka, H. (1974). *Lullaby from the womb.* Capitol.

Piaget, J. and Inhelder, B. (1969). *The psychology of the child.* New York: Basic Books.

Schaef, A. W. (1987) *When society becomes an addict.* San Francisco: Harper & Row.

Schiefelbein. S. (1986). Beginning the journey, *The incredible machine.* Washington, D.C. National Geographic Society.

APPENDIX

In the Introduction to their 1991 book, *Women's Growth in Connection,* Writings from the Stone Centre, the five women authors, while acknowledging that they cannot speak for all women, pose this fundamental challenge:

> We know that the shift we are suggesting from a psychology of "The Self" to one emphasizing relationships does not apply to women's psychology only. It points to the need for a rethinking of our study of all people.... Psychological theory, like any other cultural institution, reflects the larger Western patriarchal culture in the unexamined assumption that the white, middle class, heterosexual "paradigm man" defines not just his own reality but human reality. (p. 7)

From Chapter 1, by Dr. Jean Baker Miller, Director of Education at the Stone Centre, Wellesley College, comes this:

> The concept of the self has been prominent in psychological theory, perhaps because it has been one of the central ideas in Western thought. While various writers use different definitions, the essential idea of a "self" seems to underlie the historical development of many Western notions about such vast issues as the "good life", justice and freedom. Indeed, it seems entwined in the roots of several delineations of fundamental human motives or the highest form of existence, as in Maslow's self-actualizing character.
>
> As we have inherited it, the notion of a "self" does not appear to fit women's experience.... A question then arises, Do only men, and not women, have a self? In working with women the question is quite puzzling, but our examination of the very puzzle itself may cast new light on certain long-standing assumptions. Modern American theorists of early psychological development and, indeed, of the en-

tire life span, from Erik Erikson (1950) to Daniel Levinson (1978), tend to see all of development as a process of separating oneself out from the matrix of others— "becoming one's own man", in Levinson's words. Development of the self presumably is attained via a series of painful crises by which the individual accomplishes a sequence of allegedly essential separations from others, thereby achieving an inner sense of separated individuation. Few men ever attain such self-sufficiency, as every woman knows. They are usually supported by wives, mistresses, mothers, daughters, secretaries, nurses, and other women (as well as other men who are lower than they in the socioeconomic hierarchy). Thus, there is reason to question whether this model accurately reflects men's lives. Its goals, however, are held out for all, and are seen as the preconditions for mental health.

. . . .Thus, the prevailing models may not describe well what occurs in men: in addition, there is a question about the value of these models even if it were possible to fulfil their requirements. . . . It is very important to note, however, that the prevalent models are powerful because they have become prescriptions about what *should* happen. They accept men: they determine the actions of mental health professionals. They have affected women adversely in one way in the past. They are affecting women in another way now, if women seek "equal access" to them. Therefore, we need to examine them carefully. It is important not to embrace them because they are the only models available. (pp. 11–12)

Jordan, Judith V., Kaplan, Alexandra G., Miller, Jean Baker, Stiver, Irene P. and Surrey, Janet L. (1991). *Women's Growth in Connection.* Writings from the Stone Centre, New York: Guilford Press.

Journal of Prenatal and Perinatal Psychology and Health, 13(3–4), Spring/Summer 1999

Dying To Be Born, and Being Born To Die: Cell Death As a Defining Pattern In Human Development and Death

Christine Caldwell, Ph.D., LPC, ADTR

One of natures most elegant synchronies occurs at the doorway of our two greatest life transitions—birth and death. More precisely, the gestation process shares many parallels with the dying process, both on a cellular and an organismic level. On an organismic level we can easily note that birth and death are our two most life changing transitions—they both involve a cessation of self the way we have known it and a journey into the unknown. Both involve cataclysmic physiological changes that permanently alter us.

In the last fifty years in Western society, both birth and death have been largely relegated to hospitals, where the person undergoing this transition is frequently alone or in the hands of "experts". Their loved ones often are not blessed with bearing witness to these natural and powerful transformations. We can speculate that our lack of exposure to birth and death processes—the paucity of public support for holding and greeting a new baby, or holding and releasing a dying elder—can rob us of the spiritual growth opportunities we all need as part of our adult development. Fortunately, the synchronous rise of both the hospice and conscious birthing movements are starting to reverse this trend.

If a more microscopic look at birth and death is explored clearly it is at the cellular level where the wonder and glory begin. Death programming in the cell is essential to both fetal development and to the dying process, both of which are manifestations of an ancient evolu-

Christine Caldwell, Ph.D., LPC, ADTR, a somatic psychologist, is the founder and former director of the Somatic Psychology program at the Naropa Institute in Boulder, Colorado. She teaches and trains her work, called the Moving Cycle, internationally, and is the author of two books, *Getting Our Bodies Back*, and *Getting In Touch*. She can be reached at PO Box 19892, Boulder, CO, 80308, or at http://members.aol.com/caldwellmv.

tionary story. With sex, birth, and death on a cellular level forming the basis of our life story, we can easily see how as organisms we keep returning in open-mouthed fascination to these same archetypal sagas throughout our lives.

DEFINING DEATH ON A CELLULAR LEVEL

We can define death by peering into the process of death within the cell. Basically, our bodies are composed of two kinds of cells, the first called germ or sex cells or gametes (sperm and eggs), and somatic cells. Neese and Williams (1994) describe somatic cells as previously independent cells which devote themselves to supplying nutrients and protection to germ cells. The entire human body, in this sense, is designed just to get our gametes into the next generation! Clark (1996) points out that somatic cells when they divide don't recombine their DNA like sex cells do, and that the only purpose of somatic cells is to optimize the survival and function of the "true guardians" of the DNA, the germ cells. Simplistically, when sex cells divide, they carry half the genetic information of the parent, each gamete holding a unique, tossed-up mix of half the parents DNA. When somatic cells divide they carry all of the parent cell DNA (excluding mutations, which are also called copying errors).

Death can occur through two means—by accident, which is called *necrosis,* or through *apoptosis,* the developmental death of cells that aren't being used. Apoptosis could also be called cell suicide or senescence, a programmed sacrifice for the good of the organism, similar to death in old age. Both germ cells and somatic cells can die via *necrosis,* and have been doing so since the beginning of life. But *apoptosis* is a different story, and it is here where birth and death begin to dance together.

Early life on the planet reproduced asexually (there were no sex cells), in much the same way that cloning occurs, creating offspring cells that are essentially the same as the parent. Our somatic cells use this same billion-year-old process—liver cells creating new liver cells to replace old ones, etc. Remember, mutation does account for the slow accumulation of differences between one generation and the next, and was previously thought to be the only way that evolutionary change occurred in somatic cells.

When sexual reproduction arrived on the scene around a billion years ago and a billion years after life began (and was still largely single celled), genetic variability exploded onto the scene. By halving a cell's DNA and mixing it up with a different cell's halved DNA, evolution created a mechanism for rapid and profound adaptability to changing environments. Cellular and organismic change could occur much more rapidly because there was so much more variation for natural selection to work with, species diversification mushroomed, and life began an epic journey of increasing complexity. Fascinatingly, this tremendous new invention called sexual reproduction created the need for *apoptosis*. Death as we know it was born.

William Clark, in *Sex and the Origins of Death*, puts it this way:

> {Evolution's} drive toward ever-increasing {cell} size, and eventually multicellularity, led to the creation of extra-germinal (somatic) DNA. The advent of sex in reproduction made it necessary to destroy the somatic DNA at the end of each generation . . . Death may not be necessary for life, but programmed death is apparently necessary to realize the potential of sex as a part of reproduction. (Clark, 1966, p. 76)

Dying To Be Born

Why do somatic cells have to die? Why do organisms have to die? Apparently, because of sex and also because natural selection uses death as a way of shaping life, of keeping a glovelike fit between an organism and its environment. Charles Darwin (1859) popularized natural selection as a force that slowly caused evolution to occur over many generations, by causing less adapted organisms to leave fewer offspring or die before they reproduced. Little did he know that this same process also occurs on a cellular level on a moment to moment basis, in the developing fetus.

Gerald Edelman (1987) won the Nobel Prize for his work in cell biology. His book, *Neural Darwinism,* proposed that the nervous system of the developing fetus operated via natural selection. This idea was quite heretical at the time, for everyone assumed that evolution could only occur over many, many generations of slow genetic drift caused by the less fit of a species dying off younger and faster. Edelman came on the scene and stated that the epigenetic development of the fetus, in response to both genetic cues and environmental cues, evolved on a cellular level right in the midst of a single lifetime. What blasphemy!

To understand this process, we turn again to *apoptosis*. We tend to think of this kind of death as dying of natural causes in old age, but it is more aptly seen as cell suicide. What we now know is that all somatic cells carry within their genes a "death program," consisting of both death repressing and death promoting genes. This death programming is turned off in sex cells by death repressor genes, and under certain circumstances it is turned off in somatic cells. For instance, tumor cells have found a way to turn death repressor genes back on, or to mimic germ cells and turn death genes off. Also, *T* lymphocytes, a kind of immune cell, attack certain foreign invaders by turning on the invaders death program.

The asexual reproduction of somatic cells goes on throughout our lives—first as a way for us to grow, and then as a means of replacing cells that die via *apoptosis* or *necrosis*. This constant churning out of new cells isn't done without a few occasional copying errors (mutations). Over time, these copying errors tend to accumulate and begin to interfere with the cell doing its job (being a good liver cell, or a good blood cell, for example). As this gradual toxic accumulation occurs, it trips the cells death program, and the death program instructs the cell to commit suicide. This is our most common old age death, the suicide of a sufficient number of cells in the body that then interfere with the continuance of life.

Another process that trips the death program is when a cell fails to connect with other cells that would help it do its job, and here is where fetal development calls the shots. Very early in fetal development, embryonic cells exist in a state of totipotency. That is, the cells can become anything at first because their genome is open and all their genes are usable. As development progresses, they gradually shut down parts of their genome and therefore can only become certain cells—cells that are an expression of the remaining open genes. They travel from totipotency (I can be anything) to pluripotency (I am something in particular), and in the process they become mortal—their death program is one of the remaining open sets of genes. With their suicide programming intact, waiting to be tripped (or not) by events in the fetal environment, cell reproduction and migration roars ahead.

There is evidence that embryonic cells differentiate via cues from their location—for instance, the cells at the head of the neural tube become the brain, and the cells at the base become the spinal cord (Larsen, 1998). Where a cell ends up in relation to other cells around it determines what it will become. Location also determines whether or not its' death program will be activated. Clark (1996) points out that in the fetus cell suicide plays a crucial role in the formation of the nervous system. If a nerve fiber fails to establish a connection with an appropriate cell (and less than half do), the neuron that sent it out must commit suicide. Death is a default state for cells that fail to "web."

What determines the web? Folk wisdom in the neurosciences states that neurons that fire together, wire together. In other words, we construct our nervous system via the way it gets used initially. Still more specifically, the experiences the fetus has in its womb environment influence how its nervous system constructs itself. If a neuron connects with another cell, it will receive chemical substances called growth factors from the target cell that in effect switch off its death program. The only way the death program would get tripped again is when mutations gradually accumulate, which tends to be around eighty or so years later.

This kind of migratory life and death march in the fetus is not restricted to the nervous system. Our fingers and toes form by the death of the cells *in between* them. Immune cells are generated in excess, and only of they encounter foreign invaders will they receive growth factors which turn off their death programs. Clearly, death becomes us, even as we gestate before birth.

Conscious Evolution

What implications can we derive from this for prenatal and perinatal psychology? For myself, I never teach birth psychology without death psychology. There is no birth without death. At the same time that I teach the benefits of conscious and loving conception, gestation, birth, and bonding, I also teach the power and grace of conscious dying. I teach students to facilitate a clients recovery of their historical dimension, which I call birth work, through tracking obstructed movement sequences and finding new movement possibilities. At the same time, I teach students to facilitate a clients death work, a bodily felt experience of letting go into the unknown, also called the ultimate dimension. In this way we make our life a whole, an oscillation between finding and releasing form, where beginnings and endings merge, where birth and death become one.

Clinically, I watch for and coach a natural oscillation in my clients movement sequencing. This oscillation, I believe, represents our natural proclivity to move with *what was* and then move to *dissolve* what was. In this way the client uses body experiences to remember and acknowledge prenatal and perinatal trauma, while at the same time finding highly personal ways to move through and out of the traumas' negative imprints. We can use death to construct a new, more satisfying pattern, just like our cells do.

In between birth and death, this material implies a level of cellular consciousness that we have only intuited before. And it certainly points out that evolution is not just some epochal unfolding that gradually changes dinosaurs into birds. It is alive and well in our wombs, ovaries, and testes, and it shaped us as we lay in our mothers wombs. As pointed out by Edelman (1987), Lipton (1998), and others, evolution doesn't just work via genes differential survival into the next generation. Evolution also uses current environments to influence whether or not certain genes turn on or off, death programming genes among them. Gestational evolution is a real and happening thing. On a nuts and bolts level it alerts us to the dangers of stressful or toxic fetal environments. It may help us to understand the origins of adult suicidal feelings, and to use death imagery more consciously with these clients.

And at the same time, it may also awaken us to the possibility that we can direct our evolution more consciously, right as life begins. Lipton (1998) has enjoined us to contemplate the survival of the most loving. Now that we know that evolution occurs within our own bodies, perhaps we can use the power of love, alongside the power of movement and reproduction, as a means of consciously evolving. And being willing to die in small ways, to shape ourselves via letting go as much as efforting, will help us to access this power. Ultimately, our death will take us back into the ultimate dimension, into the mystery. Perhaps our comfort with the workings of this mystery may also dissolve the imprints of a traumatic gestation. By participating with the process of evolution as it unfolds, we embody the grace and glory that both birth and death point us towards.

REFERENCES

Clark, W. R. (1996). *Sex and the origins of death.* New York, Oxford University Press.
Darwin, C. (1859). in *The portable darwin,* Porter, D. and Graham, P., eds. New York, Penguin Books, 1993.
Edelman, G. (1987). *Neural darwinism: The theory of neuronal group selection.* New York, Basic Books.
Larsen, W. (1998). *Essentials of human embryology.* New York, Churchill Livingston.
Lipton, B. (1998). Nature, nurture, and the power of love. *Journal of Prenatal and Perinatal Psychology and Health,* 13(1), Fall 1998.
Neese, R. and Williams, G. (1995). *Why we get sick: The new science of darwinian medicine.* New York, Vintage Books.

Journal of Prenatal and Perinatal Psychology and Health, 13(3–4), Spring/Summer 1999

The Role of Childhood Memory Scores in Parenting in Pregnancy and Early Postpartum

Joann O'Leary, MS, MPH and Cecilie Gaziano, PhD, MA

ABSTRACT: As expectant parents begin the developmental tasks of pregnancy, their own histories begin to resurface, consciously or subconsciously. Ways to explore childhood memories during pregnancy in a non-threatening and nurturing way may enhance the medical care and the parenting experience in this transition. Since pregnancy is a time when people are open to new information and change, this can be an opportunity for exploring relationships with partners, their health care providers, and the unborn child. We devised a set of questions to determine what variables may interfere with the process of pregnancy, labor, birth and the postpartum period. We were interested in strengthening health care and curriculum content in birth classes for parents as they move through pregnancy and the parenting process.

THE ROLE OF CHILDHOOD MEMORY SCORES IN PARENTING IN
PREGNANCY AND EARLY POSTPARTUM

Pregnancy is the initial stage in a lifelong parenting process (Chapman, 1991; O'Leary & Thorwick, 1993; Riesch, et al, 1996; Watson, et al., 1995). People, even before conception, have expectations about the parenting experience, which are conditioned by their childhood relationships and strengthened or weakened by their present relationships (Bowlby, 1969; Findeisen, 1992; Peterson, 1992; Zeanah & Zeanah, 1989). In pregnancy, two uniquely different families come together to form another family. As expectant parents focus on the developmental tasks of pregnancy, their own histories begin to resurface, many times on an unconscious level (Belsky, 1985; O'Leary, 1992; Sa-

Joann O'Leary, MS, MPH is a parent-infant specialist at Abbott Northwestern Hospital., and Cecilie Gaziano Ph.D., is a social science consultant at Research Solutions, Inc., both of Minneapolis, Minnesota. The authors acknowledge financial support by Hennepin Technical College and Abbott Northwestern Hospital., of Minneapolis, MN, and the help of the participating parents. Address reprint requests to Joann O'Leary, Parent-Infant Specialist, Route 11605, Abbott Northwestern Hospital., 800 East 28th Street, Minneapolis, MN 55407; phone: (612) 863-4427, fax (612) 863-4615, email: joleary@allina.com.

meroff, 1994; Zeanah & Zeanah, 1989). Therefore, understanding ways to explore childhood memories during pregnancy in a non-threatening and nurturing way may enhance the medical care and the parenting experience in this transition (Coleman, Nelson, & Sundre, 1999; Onyskiw, Harrison, & Magill-Evans, 1997).

In this study we were interested in the relevance of early memories to men's and women's movement into parenthood. Our research goal was to develop a small set of measurement tools concerning past and present interpersonal relationships and positive or negative childhood memories. We wanted to improve ability to identify those expectant parents who might need extra help and support during pregnancy and after childbirth. Since pregnancy is a major life transition all parents can benefit from this process, not just those with more difficult histories.

We wanted to know which of the following variables, which previous research suggests may be relevant, were most related to negative or positive childhood memory scores, structure of families of origin (Goldenberg & Goldenberg, 1996; Unterman, Posner, & Williams, 1990; Zuckerman, et al., 1989), depressed or anxious mood (Gjerdingen, Froberg, & Fontaine, 1991; Glazer, 1989; Seguin, et al., 1995; Zaslow, et al., 1981), and social support in terms of friendship and kinship networks (Crnic, et al., 1983; Gjerdingen, et al., 1991; Seguin, et al., 1995; Zuckerman, et al., 1989), whether or not the parents were married (Pfost, Stevens, & Lum, 1990), and the strength of their attachments to their communities (Garbarino & Sherman, 1980). In addition, socioeconomic characteristics, being older, and intention to become pregnant were potentially linked to childhood memories (Pfost, Stevens, & Lum, 1990). Those with higher socioeconomic status are more likely to intend to be pregnant (Hellerstedt, et al., 1998). Further, researchers have argued increasingly for a focus on both partners (Chapman, 1991; Cronenwett & Kunst-Wilson, 1981; Ferketich & Mercer, 1995; Jordan, 1990; Nichols, 1993; Riesch, et al., 1996; Watson, et al., 1995).

The research questions were: (1) What is the relationship between childhood memory scores to variables measuring connections to others in (a) families of origin and (b) present relationships to partners, social and kin networks, and community? (2) What is the relationship, if any, between childhood memory scores and (a) anxious mood scores and (b) depressed mood scores? (3) Are childhood memory scores related to demographic variables such as age and education, as well as to intention to become pregnant? (4) Do expectant fathers and mothers differ in our measure of childhood memories?

METHOD

The participants were men and women enrolled in eight-week-long childbirth classes during the third trimester of pregnancy. Participation was voluntary. The classes were taught in a large metropolitan hospital where the babies would be born. Questionnaires were administered at four times: before classes began (n = 117), the end of classes (n = 89), babies' birth (n = 115), and one-week postpartum (n = 73). The first author distributed questionnaires in class at Times 1 and 2, and in the hospital at Time 3. Time 4 questionnaires were provided in the hospital for return by mail after one week postpartum. Results are given for those participants who completed the Time 1 and Time 4 questionnaires and who had no observations missing on relevant variables (n = 67). Findings from the second and third waves concerned other variables, which are not relevant here, except for Time 2 mood scores and fear of childbirth or labor. Some of these other results are described elsewhere (reference omitted because it would identify authors). Because the participants were self-selected, conclusions are not generalizable and apply only to the sample reported here; however, this sample was characteristic of the first-time parents in the childbirth education classes served by the hospital.

DEMOGRAPHIC AND RELATIONSHIP VARIABLES

Demographic questions included marital status, educational level, and age, among other variables. Relationships with other people were assessed by questions on number of friends and kin to whom participants felt close (based on reference omitted here so as not to identify authors), strength of ties to their communities, with whom participants lived while growing up, and whether or not their mother or primary caregiver had worked outside the home (see Appendix for wording). Participants were asked if they had been trying to get pregnant and to describe the pregnancy on a 4-point scale where "1" meant "very unpleasant" and "4" meant "very pleasant." All these variables were measured at Time 1.

CHILDHOOD MEMORY SCORES

A six-item Likert-type scale at Time 1 measured parents' memories of their own parenting experience while growing up (see Appendix).

Items were recoded to scale in the same direction with highest scores denoting the most negative memories, and they were summed to create childhood memory scores (adapted by the first author from other scales: Scott-Heyes, 1984; other reference omitted). The reliability of the memory scores was .93 (Cronbach's alpha).

MOOD SCORES

Mood scores were measured at three points, before classes began (Time 1), when they ended (Time 2), and one week postpartum (Time 4). Participants chose among 61 adjectives describing moods and feelings to indicate their feelings during the past few weeks, based on an adapted version of the Multiple Affect Adjective Check List, or MAACL (Zuckerman & Lubin, 1965). Next, each item in the anxiety series counted as "1," as did the depression words within their series. Separate scores for anxiety and depression were created by summing the appropriate items in their respective series. The MAACL contains a version of Lubin's Depression Adjective Checklist (as well as an anxiety adjective checklist), which was intended "to measure 'transient depressive mood, feeling, or emotion' (as opposed to chronic, enduring depression)" (Shaver & Brennan, 1991, p. 215). These scales do not rely on clinical diagnoses and have the advantage of being short and easily understood. They are a tool with which a wide variety of professionals can work without clinical training as psychologists or psychiatrists. Reliabilities (Cronbach's alpha) were high and comparable to others reported in the literature (Shaver & Brennan, 1991; Zuckerman & Lubin, 1965), .79 for anxiety scores and .83–.85 for depression. (Although having a cesarean birth might affect mothers' or fathers' psychological states, birth outcomes were not related to mood scores on depression or anxiety at one week postpartum.)

ANTICIPATION AND EVALUATION OF CHILDBIRTH AND LABOR

Affective anticipation of childbirth was measured by a six-item scale including fearfulness, being afraid, nervous, worried, calm, confident, and excited. Two other six-item scales measured anticipated evaluation of labor and of birth using the same semantic differentials as the childhood memory score. These scales were based on Scott-Heyes (1984) and are given in the Appendix also.

Statistical Tests. Preliminary analyses included Pearson and Spearman correlation analyses, cross-tabulations, t-tests, and an analysis of variance. The variables with the greatest magnitudes of relationship with memory scores then were entered as independent variables in a multiple regression on childhood memory scores as the dependent variable.

RESULTS

Research participants did not differ significantly by gender on demographics, family of origin, or intention to conceive (Table 1). According to t-tests (data not shown), gender made little or no difference in number of relatives or friends to whom participants felt close, strength of community ties, most of the mood scores, and perceived pleasantness of pregnancy. Women tended to have slightly higher Time 1 anxiety mood scores and Time 4 depression mood scores than did men. While gender made significant differences in five of nine evaluations and anticipation of childbirth and labor, these measures had little or no correlation with childhood memory scores in general (discussed further below). Since gender had little association with the main variables of interest, the participants were combined into one group for analysis. (Participants also had been analyzed as dyads, measuring difference in scores and other variables with no significant differences found.)

About 6 women in 10 were less than 30 years old, and the men were slightly older, overall (Table 1). Participants were well educated, compared to the general metropolitan population, and the women tended to be a little more educated than the men. About 8 in 10 expectant parents were married and living together. Compared to participants at Time 1, those participants who dropped out of the study by Time 4 were disproportionately more likely to be older, married, less educated, and to have intended the pregnancy (data not shown).

One-third of research participants anticipated moving away from their present community within the next ten years; the rest had no plans to move. Most participants had grown up primarily in homes with both parents present. Overall, they divided roughly into one-third whose mothers or primary caregivers had never worked for pay, one-third whose mothers had worked part time while participants were growing up, and one-third whose mothers had been employed full time. The women's mothers were more likely to have worked full time than were the men's mothers (n.s.).

Table 1
Expectant Parents' Demographic and Relationship Characteristics

Independent Variable	Women (n = 35) (%)	Men (n=32) (%)	Total (n=67) (%)
Age			
Younger than 30 years old	59[a]	53	56
30 years of age or older	41	47	44
Education			
High school graduate or less	9[a]	19	14
Attended college/not graduate	18	15	17
College graduate	50	47	49
Graduate work beyond college degree	23	19	21
Marital status			
Married	80	81	81
Not married, separated, live apart	20	19	19
Had been trying to become pregnant			
Yes	57	56	57
No	43	44	43
Length of community residence expected			
Ten years or less time	33	32[b]	33
More than ten years	67	68	67
With whom participants lived while growing up			
Lived with both parents	86	91	88
Lived with one parent or others	14	9	12
Employment of mother/primary caregiver			
Worked full time	43	28	36
Worked part time	29	34	31
Never worked outside the home	29[c]	38	33

[a]1 female case missing.
[b]1 male case missing.
[c]Does not sum to 100% because of rounding.

Table 2
T-tests on Childhood Memory Scores by Independent
Variables Measuring Connections to Others

Independent Variable	Childhood Memory Scores		
	Mean	S.D.	n
Length of expected residence in communities			
Ten years or less time	18.29*	6.82	21
More than ten years	13.95	7.05	42
With whom participants lived while growing up			
Lived with both parents	14.34**	6.73	59
Lived with one parent			
or others	22.86	6.34	7
Had been trying to become pregnant			
Yes	13.45*	7.29	38
No	17.68	6.28	28

Note: Cases missing values excluded, total n = 67.
*p < .05, two-tailed test.
**p < .01, two-tailed test.

CHILDHOOD MEMORY SCORES

The women had a mean childhood memory score of 14.71 points (s.d. = 6.99), and the men's mean score was slightly more negative (15.84, s.d. = 7.39), a nonsignificant difference (t-value = .64). The remaining analyses on childhood memory scores were based on total group (mean = 15.24, s.d. = 7.15). More negative childhood memory scores were associated significantly with expecting to move from one's community within the next ten years, growing up in one-parent households, and unplanned pregnancies, according to t-tests (Table 2).

Full-time employment of respondents' primary caregivers while respondents were growing up was associated with negative childhood memory scores, according to analysis of variance (Table 3). Part-time or non-employment made less difference in memory scores. Participants from homes lacking two parents were more likely to have had a mother or other primary caregiver who worked full time for pay.

Having fewer relatives to whom participants felt close, weaker community ties, higher mood scores on depression and anxiety, and more negative perceptions of the pregnancy made significant differences in childhood memory scores (Table 4). Having fewer close friends also

Table 3
Analysis of Variance on Childhood Memory Scores by Primary Caregiver's Employment

Independent Variable	Childhood Memory Scores		
	Mean	S.D.	n
Employment status of mother or primary caregiver most of the time while participants were growing up			
Worked full time	19.00	7.31	24
Worked part time	12.40	5.37	20
Never employed	13.73	6.86	22
Total	15.24	7.14	66[a]

Analysis of Variance:

Source of Variation	Sums of Squares	Degrees of Freedom	Mean Square	F	Sig. of F
Between groups	550.96	2	275.48	6.27	.01
Within groups	2767.16	63	43.92		
Total	3318.12	65[b]			

[a]1 case missing.
[b]2 cases missing.

made a difference, although nonsignificant. Among the men, fearful anticipation of labor and childbirth was positively correlated with childhood memory scores (r = .34, 2-tailed p (.06, n = 31) at Time 1 (before the beginning of the eight-week prenatal class) and at Time 3 (as soon as possible after childbirth) (r = .32, 2-tailed p (.10, n = 28). Negative evaluations of what it is like to give birth at Time 3 had the highest correlation with negative childhood memory scores among the men (r = .53, 2-tailed p (.01, n = 30). Among the women, fear of childbirth and negative perceptions of childbirth or labor were uncorrelated with negative childhood memories or correlations were non-significant.

Anxiety and depression mood scores correlated most highly with negative childhood memory scores at Time 4 (.40 and .26, respectively). Correlations of Time 1 and Time 2 anxiety scores with childhood memory scores were of smaller magnitude those at Time 4 (.27 and .13, respectively). Part correlations were modest, and partial correlations were very low. Time 1 and Time 2 depression mood scores cor-

Table 4
Pearson Correlations of Childhood Memory Scores With
Variables Measuring Connections to Others

Scores	Correlation with Childhood Memory n	Independent Variables
Number of relatives to whom participants feel close	−0.30**	59
Number of friends to whom participants feel close	−0.17	59
Strength of community ties	−0.21*	65
Mood scores on depression at one week postpartum (Time 4)	0.26*	59
Mood scores on anxiety at one week postpartum (Time 4)	0.40**	59
Describe pregnancy as pleasant on a scale of "1 to 4" where "1" means "very unpleasant" and "4" means "very pleasant"	−0.33**	63

Note: Cases missing values excluded (total n = 67).
*p < .05, two-tailed test.
**p < .01, two-tailed test.

related with negative childhood memory scores at .16 and .13, respectively; their part and partial correlations with memory scores were very low (.06 or less).

The variables which showed the strongest associations with childhood memory scores were entered as independent variables into a stepwise multiple regression analysis on childhood memory scores. The following variables were retained in the regression equation: anxiety scores at Time 4 (one week postpartum), living with only one parent or with other caregivers while growing up (dummy variable coded 1 for both parents and 0 for one parent or other), and having fewer relatives to whom participants felt close (Table 5). The number of participants who had not grown up in two-parent families was small, however.

Table 5
Stepwise Multiple Regression Results: Independent Variables and Childhood Memory Scores as Dependent Variable

Predictor	B	se	Beta	se	p<
Anxiety scores at one week postpartum	0.63	0.20	0.34	0.11	.01
Family of origin structure (with whom participants lived while growing up) (dummy variable coded 1 = both parents, 0 = 1 parent/ neither)	−6.93	2.46	−0.30	0.11	.01
Number of relatives to whom participants feel close	−0.59	0.27	−0.23	0.11	.05
Constant	21.29	3.02			.001
Multiple R	0.57				
R2		0.32			
Adjusted R2	0.29				

Note: n = 64, 3 cases missing.

DISCUSSION

The first author devised a scale for measuring positive and negative childhood memories, which was compared with direct and indirect indicators of relationships with others. The research aim was to select variables which were the most correlated with negative childhood memories to help guide, not only health educators in strengthening curriculum, but also assist providers in asking questions that might impact health care. While this will help identify parents who may need more support, all parents can benefit from exploring family of origin issues during pregnancy and postpartum as they take on the parenting role.

The variables most related to negative childhood memory scores were high anxiety mood scores at one week postpartum, growing up in a household lacking one or both parents, and having few relatives to whom research participants felt close. These three variables explained 30% of the variance in childhood memory scores. Other variables which were significantly related to childhood memory scores included marital status, strength of community attachment, intention to conceive, perceived pleasantness of pregnancy, and depression mood scores. Size of friendship networks made a small, nonsignificant difference. The relationships between childhood memory scores and mood scores on anxiety and depression increased between the beginning of childbirth education classes and postpartum. This might possibly be due to the emotional feelings that surface after the birth of a baby which cannot be anticipated until a parent reaches that point.

Gender had little or no impact on childhood memory scores, connections to family and others, and mood scores, underscoring the utility of studying these concepts in both parents. On the other hand, negative childhood memory scores were linked to fearful anticipation of childbirth or labor, as well as to negative evaluations of labor and birth, in the men in this study but not the women with respect to one Time 1 measurement and two Time 3 measurements. These findings are of interest because spouses are the major, often only, source of emotional support for adult men (Cronenwett & Kunst-Wilson, 1981). Pregnancy can precipitate major reworking of men's past and present relationships with their fathers, mothers, siblings, and wives, as well as their sense of self (Gurwitt, 1976). The results support calls for further work to investigate the needs of expectant and new fathers (Ferketich & Mercer, 1995; Glazer, 1989). Just helping fathers focus on the needs of mothers during labor and birth does not prepare them to assume the fathering role (Chapman, 1991; Jordan, 1990; Nichols, 1993; Watson, et al., 1995).

LIMITATIONS OF THE STUDY

The expectant parents in our study were self-selected and more educated than the population at large. They were, however, representative of the population which the childbirth education classes serve. Their patterns are not generalizable to other settings and populations. Additional research should be undertaken, especially in larger samples employing randomization. Additional indicators of relationships to family, friends, and community are desirable to improve measurement and concept development. More variables should be studied, as well, to increase prediction and understanding of the relationships involve.

IMPLICATIONS FOR PRACTITIONERS AND EDUCATORS

Since pregnancy is a time when people are open to new information and change (Nugent & Brazelton, 1989), childbirth classes are an ideal setting for exploring relationships with partners, with their health care providers, and with the unborn child. The same content can be presented in a framework of how it fits for each individual family. Exploring how each partner's family background may be different can help resolve issues that they may not know about each other. Breastfeeding may be a strong value for one partner and something not discussed in another family. Discussing how expectant parents learned to get their needs met when growing up can be part of comfort measures in labor and whether they may want pain medication or not, depending on the value systems of their family of origins. Exploring childhood memories with people leads into what tools they can use now in labor and birth or what resources they may need to seek out for further support. Rather than being upset with a partner who can't give support, some partners may seek out the use of a doula in labor to compliment and strengthen what each person has brought into the pregnancy.

Amount of social support during pregnancy and the relationship with a significant other are key variables in most research on adaptation to pregnancy (Crnic, et al., 1983; Gjerdingen, et al., 191; Seguin, et al., 1995; Zuckerman, et al., 1989). Isolation can be a major cause of depression. Bringing home a new baby without social support can be both isolating and overwhelming. When new parents have had childhoods lacking outside resources for support, or they did not learn how to reach out to others when in need, they may find it very difficult to know how to ask for help. New mothers and fathers provided with a realistic picture of the emotional stages of becoming a parent and that the first three months of life is the phase of attachment readiness (Eagan, 1985), learn that the disequilibrium of postpartum adjustment are normal and predictable. They also can learn what resources are available to aid them in their communities.

These results demonstrate the utility of childhood memory scores and indicators of past and present relationships as a tool for professionals assisting people as they move through pregnancy and postpartum, as well as for identifying men and women who might have more difficulty. Some parents may need more follow up than others. In addition, related research has found that negative childhood memories and perceptions of poor treatment by parents are related to more difficult labor and birth experiences and more negative attitudes toward pregnancy (Peterson, 1992). The first author's experience in facilitating postpartum groups through the first four months is that face-to-face interaction with their babies brings back parents' own family of origin experiences. A group setting is a safe place to process past issues because all the new parents are having similar experiences to some degree. All the participants are undergoing the same transition. Those with more negative childhood memories may feel more accepting of further help when they realize much of what they are feeling is normal for all people. They are then more able to identify their own behaviors that are deviant from normal and seek help for themselves.

People's perceptions of how to be a parent begin in their own early childhoods when they are formulating their notions of how to have relationships, and the process of transmitting models of relationships recurs from generation to generation (Goldenberg & Goldenberg, 1996; Zeanah & Zeanah, 1989). Many parents need to be aware that they are going to have more trouble with adjustment and need to seek support, especially if they are more isolated from social networks, grew up in families which were not intact, and are at risk for higher mood scores on depression and anxiety. The birth of a child and the accompanying infant caregiving tasks initiate the need for parents to reorganize their relationships, both past and present.

REFERENCES

Belsky, J. (1985). Experimenting with the family in the newborn period. *Child Development*, 56, 407–414.

Bowlby, J. (1969). Attachment and loss: Vol. 1. Attachment. New York: Basic Books.

Chapman, L. (1991). Expectant fathers' roles during labor and birth. *JOGNN*, 21, 114–120.

Coleman, P., Nelson, E. S., & Sundre, D. L. (1999). The relationship between prenatal expectations and postnatal attitudes among first-time mothers. *Journal of Reproductive and Infant Psychology*, 17, 27–39.

Crnic, K. A., Greenberg, M. T., Ragozin, A. S., Robinson, N. M., & Basham, R. B. (1983). Effects of stress and social support on mothers and premature and full term infants. *Child Development*, 54, 209–217.

Cronenwett, L. R., & Kunst Wilson, W. (1981). Stress, social support, and the transition to fatherhood. *Nursing Research*, 30, 196–201.

Eagan, A. B. (1985). The Newborn Mother: Stages of Her Growth. Boston: Little, Brown.

Ferketich, S. L., & Mercer, R. T. (1985). Predictors of role competence for experienced and inexperienced fathers. *Nursing Research*, 44, 89–95.

Findeisen, B. (1992). The long term psychological impact of pre- and perinatal experiences. Presentation at the World Congress of Prenatal and Perinatal Psychology and Medicine. Kracow, Poland. In *International Journal of Prenatal & Perinatal Studies*, 4, Supplement 1, 14.

Garbarino, J., & Sherman, D. (1980). High risk neighborhoods and high risk families: The human ecology of child maltreatment. *Child Development*, 51, 188–198.

Gjerdingen, D. K., Froberg, D. G., & Fontaine, P. (1991). The effects of social support on women's health during pregnancy, labor and delivery, and the postpartum period. *Family Medicine*, 23, 370–375.

Glazer, G. (1989). Anxiety and stressors of expectant fathers. *Western Journal of Nursing Research*, 11, 47–59.

Goldenberg, I., & Goldenberg, H. (1996). Family Therapy: An Overview (4th ed.). Pacific Grove, CA, Brooks/Cole.

Gurwitt, A. R. (1976). Aspects of prospective fatherhood: A case report. *Psychoanalytic Study of the Child,* 31, 237–271.

Hellerstedt, W. L., Pirie, P. L., Lando, H. A., Curry, S. J., McBride, C. M., Grothaus, L. C., & Nelson, J. C. (1998). Differences in preconceptional and prenatal behaviors in women with intended and unintended pregnancies. *American Journal of Public Health,* 88, 663–666.

Jordan, P. L. (1990). Laboring for relevance: expectant and new fatherhood. *Nursing Research,* 39, 11–16.

Nichols, M. R. (1993). Paternal perspectives of the childbirth experience. *Maternal & Child Nursing Journal,* 21, 99–108.

Nugent, J. K., & Brazelton, T. B. (1989). Preventive intervention with infants and families: The NBAS model. *Infant Mental Health Journal,* 10, 84–94.

O'Leary, J. M. (1992). Parenting during pregnancy: A developmental theory. *Pre- and Perinatal Psychology Journal,* 7, 113–123.

O'Leary, J., & Thorwick, C. (1993). Parenting during pregnancy: The infant as the vehicle for intervention in high risk pregnancy. *International Journal of Prenatal and Perinatal Psychololgy and Medicine,* 5, 303–310.

Onyskiw, J. E., Harrison, M. J., & Magill-Evans, J. E. (1997). Past childhood experiences and current parent-infant interactions. *Western Journal of Nursing Research,* 19, 501–518.

Peterson, G. (1992). A preventive prenatal counseling model. In R. Klimek (Ed.), *Pre and Perinatal Psychology and Medicine.* Krakow, Poland.

Pfost, K. S., Stevens, M. J., & Lum, C. U. (1990). The relationship of demographic variables, antepartum depression, and stress to postpartum depression. *Journal of Clinical Psychology,* 46, 588–592.

Riesch, S. K., Kuester, L., Brost, D., & McCarthy, J. G. (1996). Fathers' perceptions of how they were parented. *Journal of Community Health Nursing,* 13, 13–29.

Sameroff, A. J. (1994). Developmental systems and family functioning. In R. D. Parke & S. G. Kellan (Eds.), *Exploring Family Relationships with Other Social Contexts* (pp. 199–224). Hillsdale, NJ, Erlbaum.

Scott Heyes, G. (1984). Childbearing as a mutual experience. Unpublished doctoral dissertation, New University of Ulster, Northern Ireland.

Seguin, L., Potvin, L., St. Denis, M., & Loiselle, J. (1995). Chronic stressors, social support, and depression during pregnancy. *Obstetrics & Gynecology,* 85, 583–589.

Shaver, P. R., & Brennan, K. A. (1991). Measures of depression and loneliness, in Robinson, J. P., Shaver, P. R., & Wrightsman, L. S. (Eds.). *Measures of Personality and Social Psychological Attitudes* (pp. 195–289, see especially pp. 215–219). San Diego, Academic Press.

Unterman, R. R., Posner, N. A., & Williams, K. N. (1990). Postpartum depressive disorders: changing trends. *Birth,* 131–137.

Watson, W. J, Watson, L., Wetzel, W., Bader, E., & Talbot, Y. (1995). Transition to parenthood. What about fathers? *Canadian Family Physician,* 41, 807–812.

Zaslow, M., Pederson, F., Kramer, E., Cain, R., Suwalsky, J., & Fivel, M. (1981). Depressed Mood in New Fathers: Interviews and Behavioral Correlates. Boston, Society for Research in Child Development.

Zeanah, C. H., & Zeanah, P. D. (1989). Intergenerational transmission of maltreatment: Insights from attachment theory and research. *Psychiatry,* 52, 177–196.

Zuckerman, B., Amaro, H., Bauchner, H., & Cabral, H. (1989). Depressive symptoms during pregnancy: relationship to poor health behaviors. *American Journal of Obstetrics & Gynecology,* 160(5-Pt 1), 1107–1111.

Zuckerman, M., & Lubin, B. (1965). Manual for the Multiple Affect Adjective Check List. San Diego, CA, Educational and Industrial Testing Service.

APPENDIX

A. The pregnancy:

Q1. Had you been trying to get pregnant?

 a. Yes 1
 b. No...2

Q2. How would you describe the pregnancy so far?

 a. Very unpleasant 1
 b. Unpleasant...2
 c. Pleasant...3
 d. Very pleasant 4

B. Anticipation of labor and birth:

Q3. You probably have some idea what it will be like to give birth. How do you feel now when you think about you [your partner's] labor and giving birth? Please circle the number for each adjective below which comes closest to how you feel. (From Scott-Heyes, 1984)

	Not at all	Slightly	Somewhat	Very much
a. Afraid	1	2	3	4
*b. Calm	1	2	3	4
*c. Confident	1	2	3	4
*d. Excited	1	2	3	4
e. Nervous	1	2	3	4
f. Worried	1	2	3	4

*Recode items to scale in the opposite direction, so highest score = more negative anticipation.

C. Evaluation of labor and birth:

Q4. Now, we'd like to ask what you think your [your partner's] labor will be like. Some words which are opposites are shown below with a scale from "1 to 7," on which "1" and "7" are the most extreme, "4" is in the middle, and the other numbers fall in between. Please circle the number below which is closest to what you think your [your partner's] labor will be like.

a. Good	1	2	3	4	5	6	7	Bad
*b. Painful	1	2	3	4	5	6	7	Painless
c. Happy	1	2	3	4	5	6	7	Unhappy
*d. Sick	1	2	3	4	5	6	7	Healthy
e. Pleasant	1	2	3	4	5	6	7	Unpleasant
*f. Uncomfortable	1	2	3	4	5	6	7	Comfortable

*Recode items to scale in the opposite direction, so highest score = more negative anticipation.

Q5. And what do you think the birth will be like? Here, "the birth" refers only to the time from when the top of the baby's head can first be seen until he or she is completely born. (From Scott-Heyes, 1984) [REPEAT THE PREVIOUS SCALE, GOOD-BAD, ETC.]

D. Relationships with others: Now, here are some questions about you and your family:

Q6. How many close friends do you have (people that you feel at ease with, can talk to about private matters, and can call on for help)?

PLEASE CIRCLE ONE: 0 1 2 3 4 5 6 7 8 9 10 (or more)

Q7. How many relatives do you have that you feel close to?

PLEASE CIRCLE ONE: 0 1 2 3 4 5 6 7 8 9 10 (or more)

Q8. With whom did you live for the majority of the time until you were 18 years old?

```
    a. Both mother and father ....................................... 1
    b. Mother only ...................................................... 2
    c. Father only ....................................................... 3
    d. Other (please specify:) _____ 4
```

Q9. When you were growing up, did your mother (or female guardian) work outside the home at any time either full time or part time, or did she never work outside the home?

```
    a. Full time............................................................ 1
    b. Part time........................................................... 2
    c. Never worked outside the home ........................... 3
```

Q10. Now picture a scale from "1 to 10," where "10" stands for someone who has strong ties to his or her local community and would strongly prefer to continue living there, while "1" stands for someone without any ties to the local community and would not be reluctant to move away. Where would you place yourself on that scale?

PLEASE CIRCLE ONE: 0 1 2 3 4 5 6 7 8 9 10 (or more)

Q11. How long have you lived in the community in which you reside now?

    a. 5 years or less 1
    b. Between 6 and 10 years..................................2
    c. Between 11 and 20 years 3
    d. More than 20 years 4

Q12. How long do you plan to remain in this community?

    a. 5 years or less 1
    b. Between 6 and 10 years..................................2
    c. Between 11 and 20 years 3
    d. More than 20 years 4

E. Childhood memory score:

Q13. So much of how we parent comes from our own background experience. Please describe your own memory of how you were parented. Some words which are opposites are shown below with a scale from "1 to 7," on which "1" and "7" are the most extreme and the other numbers fall in between. Please circle the number below which is closest to how you think you were parented.

a. Good	1	2	3	4	5	6	7	Bad
*b. Painful	1	2	3	4	5	6	7	Painless
c. Happy	1	2	3	4	5	6	7	Unhappy
*d. Sick	1	2	3	4	5	6	7	Healthy
e. Pleasant	1	2	3	4	5	6	7	Unpleasant
*f. Uncomfortable	1	2	3	4	5	6	7	Comfortable

*Recode items to scale in the opposite direction, so highest score = more negative memory score.

F. Mood scores:

Q14. Below are some words which describe different kinds of moods and feelings. Please circle the number of the words below which describe how you have been feeling in the last few weeks. Some of the words may sound alike, but each one is a little different from the others. Please circle all of the numbers corresponding to the words which describe your feelings. Please work quickly.

[For list of words, see: Zuckerman & Lubin (contains both anxiety and depression mood scales), 1965, or Shaver & Brennan, 1991 (depressive mood scale only).]

Journal of Prenatal and Perinatal Psychology and Health, 13(3–4), Spring/Summer 1999

SHARING SPACE

I. Fathers Are an Essential Part of the Human Environment

Patrick Gallagher

I always knew I'd be a father. I don't know how I knew, but as far back as I can recall, I knew that I would grow up and have children. I remember the day that my wife told me that she was definitely pregnant. We were sitting outside on a hot August day. I remember the green grass, the leaves on the bushes, the breeze, and the agitation in my body. I remember sitting back—this I remember best of all— and feeling that the axis of the universe had shifted; I was almost dizzy from it. From that moment on nothing was the same. I was a new man. The concerns of the old man were irrelevant—important in their day, but that day was done. Everything I would do I would now do as a father, as a man responsible for bringing a new world to birth. I felt a powerful need for some kind of purification ritual, something that symbolized the end of the old universe and the beginning of the new. But there is no such ritual. Being a father, being a parent, is considered a private act.

It's almost eleven years since then, and I am now a father three times. I was right that day. The universe did shift on its axis, everything was new, the old world was gone, and a new one born.

My experiences are what most fathers experience: the unparalleled joy of holding your new child; the terrible certainty that you will make mistakes; the longing to protect; the regret of missed opportunities; the shameful pain of admitting to failure—again; the desperate fear that your sick child might die; the wonder of realizing that your bond with your wife will not only last as long as you both live, but beyond.

Being a father has been the greatest, most challenging, most excit-

Patrick Gallagher is a book editor in Toronto, Ontario and the father of three children. His article was first published in *Catholic New Times*. Reprinted by permission.

ing experience of my life. It has transformed me and made me. I can think of no other calling that could be as deeply satisfying to a man.

But I fear for the generation growing up. I feel anxious for my own two sons. What will fatherhood mean to them? What messages are they hearing about being a father? Will they want to be fathers?

The answers are not reassuring, because fatherhood, indeed parenthood, is in crisis. Although most fathers, Re me, are struggling to do their best in a society in which human connections and solidarity are increasingly tenuous and frayed, the public face of fatherhood has become sadly disfigured.

When was the last time that you read or heard of fathering discussed as a noble or valuable task? If you are a father, can you recall the last time that what you do was presented or talked about in a way that made you feel supported rather than undermined?

There seem to be two images of fathers today. The first is of a bumbling fool, a man less mature than his children, patronized by his wife, incompetent in anything that matters. This caricature can be found on television, in movies, on radio and in advertising The epitome of this father is Ed Bundy, *Married With Children,* though his imitators are legion.

The second image is that of an indifferent, irresponsible, selfish brute, a virtual psychopath seeking with low cunning for the opportunity to abuse his wife and children. These are the fathers portrayed in countless newspaper and magazine articles, in popular movie-of-the-week television shows, in novels and films.

I know that some fathers abuse or abandon their wives and children; I know that some fathers are not mature or very responsible. But these are examples of fatherhood gone wrong. They reveal the pathology of fatherhood, not its nature. Yet the pathology is, I fear, fast becoming the norm in the public mind. Social policy debates either exclude fathers (mothers are not treated much better) or consider them a harmful influence. Women now seriously contemplate having a child without the child having a father, as though the only effect of this will be a slightly heavier burden of child care and domestic maintenance.

Humans live in families like fish live in water. It is the environment that surrounds and nourishes them. Acid rain, untreated sewage, human carelessness and indifference all pollute lakes and rivers and make them unfit for fish to live in. Yet no one would suggest that we should breed fish that can live in garbage or that we should remove fish from water and treat them as though they were mammals.

In the last half of the 20th century families have also become polluted; from the untreated sewage of a social and political system that treats people callously and cruelly; from the acid rain of cynicism and despair; and from human indifference and carelessness. Why do we then undermine and degrade further the world we are born into and must we live in if we are to thrive? Why do we not support this primary social nexus as it attempts its necessary task against overpowering odds?

Ironically, we seem to have awakened to the mysteriousness and fragility of the living habitats of animal species—except for one. Fathers are an essential part of the human environment. Without the charisma of fathering in our lives, all of us—men, women, and children are diminished. We will be incomplete.

Yet, I remain, if not optimistic, at least hopeful. Social forces are powerful, but not quite as powerful as a loving individual. I look around and see lots of men attempting sometimes successfully, sometimes not, sometimes with ease, sometimes with difficulty, to be good fathers. They are, for the most part, invisible, their efforts validated only by the response of their children, to whom the future belong.

2.   The Infant's Questions

Lee Carroll

The human mother was startled indeed when the large male angel appeared in her laundry room. "What are you doing here?"

"You expected me in the kitchen?" asked the angel.

"No, I didn't expect you at all!" the mother answered. "Why are you here?"

"To grant your request," said the angel, as if it were a common thing to appear in a human's home.

"I don't remember any request!" exclaimed the mother. "I hope I asked for something good and that you didn't just overhear me swearing. I say things all the time when I'm mad."

"No, no," replied the angel. "Remember when you were looking into the eyes of your son and murmured, *If only we could talk to each other?* Well, I'm here to arrange that. Tomorrow night when you go into your son's nursery, I will be there to allow you to speak to him, and he to you. You will have a brief time where he can speak to you with the

From *The Parables of Kryon* by Lee Carroll (1996). Carlsbad, CA: Hay House, Inc. Reprinted with permission of Lee Carroll and Hay House.

intellect of an adult and the language of an adult. I'll tell you more when I see you then." And with that, the angel disappeared—slightly to the left of the dryer—and up a vent.

The mother was not frightened. After all, she believed in angels and had been to the local angel shop many times. She had no way of knowing that real angels don't like angel shops. All the popularity had taken the fun out of appearing before people. Some mothers even wanted to know where the angel got its costume—very insulting to a real live angel.

The mother didn't sleep much that night, and when she put her six-month-old infant to bed early in the evening, she looked deep into his eyes and said, "Tomorrow, you and I will actually get to speak to each other!" She was excited indeed. He drooled in response.

She carefully crafted what she would say to him. Where does one begin? How long would she have? Would she be able to communicate the difficult things of life? She started by thinking of all the things she wanted to tell a child just starting out in life—about how a stove is hot, and a pretty fire can hurt—but wait! The angel said the child would speak with an adult's mind. That would change everything! She would need to tell him how to handle girls, and how to treat a broken heart, and how not to trust everyone, and how not to drive too fast. Oh my! There is so much to tell him about being human, she thought.

The next evening, the time for the magic discussion slowly approached. She waited with her infant son at her side in the nursery until the appointed hour, when the angel appeared again.

"Nice to see both of you," the angel quickly said. "Here are the rules of the conversation. Mom, you can only answer. Son, you can only ask three questions. Then it's over." And with that, the angel again disappeared—this time down the furnace grate.

This changes everything, thought the mother in silence while looking at her son. Perhaps I am hallucinating. I'll bet my son simply goes to sleep now. Instead, the infant stood up!

"Mother," said the infant. "it's a magical day indeed that brings us together like this. What a joy to be able to speak to you at this point in my life!"

The mother stood up at attention—with her mouth dropping in amazement. She even drooled a bit.

"Only three questions can I ask," the boy continued from the crib. "I want to know so much!" The boy was thinking about his first question as his mother was taking it all in. This is real, she thought. My son is talking to me as if he were all grown up! What a miracle. What a gift. She could hardly contain herself waiting for her son's first question. Would it be about philosophy or religion? Perhaps he would want to know the best advice to guide him into a good career, or maybe he wanted to know how he should choose the best mate—one who would stick around longer than hers did. The boy looked into his mother's eyes and asked the first question.

"Mother, I have laid outside this house on my back and was amazed at the sky. Why is it blue?"

It was all the mother could do not to shout: "You wasted the first question! Who cares why the sky is blue!" But the mother was so in love with her son that she patiently answered the question according to the rules. She explained how the atmosphere and oxygen molecules refract the light of the sun and turn it blue—at least that's what she believed. It sounded good, anyway. She anxiously waited for the next question. The next one has to be better, she thought. Perhaps he would like to know what he should do with his life in order not to end up homeless or with delinquent friends.

"Mother, my second question is this. Although I have been here only six months, I notice that sometimes it is hot outside, and sometimes it is cold. Why is that?"

The mother was appalled. Another question wasted on dumb stuff! How could this be, she wondered. Her son was innocent and alert. His question was important to him, and she treasured this magic time they could have together. Slowly, she tried to tell him about the Earth and the sun, and how the Earth tilts slightly as it orbits the sun, causing winter and summer, cold and hot. Finally, it was time for the last question. They had been at it for almost thirty minutes, and so little had actually been communicated.

"Mother, I love you!" exclaimed the son. "But how do I know you are really my mother? Do you have some kind of proof?"

What kind of a question was this? Where did that come from? Who else would be his mother? Hadn't she cared for him every day of his life? What a disappointment this session had been. She almost wanted to walk away and go back to the laundry room where this had all started. She thought of how she was going to shove the angel in the dryer the next time she saw him. Her son, his innocent eyes wide open and alert, was waiting for a reply.

She started crying, but held out her hands and said, "Look at my fingers; they are just like yours. My feet and my face look like yours. My expressions of joy and love are just like yours. I am truly your mother. We have the same eyes and mouth—look!" With that, the child was satisfied, and he slowly laid himself down on his mat and went to sleep.

That was it? This miracle of communication had come and gone, and the mother had not had a meaningful conversation with her beautiful son. What happened? What went wrong? She spent a great deal of time thinking about it all, and she mourned the passing of such an event without anything substantive being transferred.

Then the angel appeared again—up through the bathroom drain.

"Go away," the mother said before the angel could say anything. "What a disappointment you turned out to be."

"I gave you the time," the angel said kindly. "I did not design the questions."

"What good was it? Why didn't my son ask anything important? You told me he would have the mind of an adult, but he asked the questions of a child. You have tricked me with your so-called miracle."

"Dear one," the angel replied, "although your son was given the language and the intellect of an adult, he had only the wisdom and experience of the six months he had been on Earth. His questions were therefore the most meaningful ones he could think of, and you answered them all. Even the last one, which was postured in fear, you answered correctly. In addition, you transmitted your love to him while you were together, and you were not impatient with him. He did his best and was honest. What more could you ask?"

The mother sat down. She hadn't thought of that. Her son had mustered up the best questions he could come up with. How could he know what to ask if he didn't have the wisdom she had? And if he had somehow been given that wisdom, he would not have had to ask anything! Without any more communication, the angel left for the final time—this time out the window.

The mother returned to the crib and spent a long time looking at her precious son. "You did your best, my son," she said in a quiet voice. "It was good that we had time for a talk."

3.   The First Cesarean Birth

Jane English, Ph.D.

In a cave part way up the side of a valley a small group of people sit around an open fire. It is early spring at the end of a long hard winter. Several members of this small band of people have died during the winter. The others are weak but glad to see the beginnings of spring.

Based on the shamanic journey experience of Jane English in 1984. The author's email address is: <jenglish@macshasta.com>

Until this night they had also been happy about the imminent birth of a child to one of the women. But the mood is somber as they sit around the fire. For the woman lying on some furs is near death after a long hard labor. The child has not been born. It seems that not only is there not to be a birth but that there will be one more death. The band is getting so small it may not survive.

Across the fire from where the young woman lies is an older woman whose hair is beginning to gray. She is the keeper of the knowledge of herbs for this band and is consulted in all health matters. She suddenly sits up straighter and peers intently at the younger woman lying there. She can see no movement of breathing; perhaps death has already come.

Reaching into her leather pouch for an obsidian stone she uses for cutting leather, she stands and silently walks toward the young woman. Telepathically she communicates to the young woman not to be afraid. She sees that the woman's soul has indeed left the body and is hovering there above the fire.

Gently the older woman pulls aside the furs and leather dress covering the young woman's belly. Carefully she cuts open the belly a layer at a time, finds the head of the child, and lifts it out. By now other women have come to assist her as she delivers the child. All are awed, some are afraid, but they trust the older woman.

The child cries and breathes jerkily as the women clean him off and wrap him in soft furs. The older woman motions another young woman who is the mother of a one-year-old to take the newborn and nurse him.

The older woman puts herbs, maybe sage, into the wound and thanks the great earth-mother-goddess for this new life and for the vision of how to safely deliver the baby from its dead mother's body. Perhaps the older woman remembered seeing living baby rabbits come from the cut open belly of a pregnant rabbit whom the woman had killed with a rock from her sling.

This small band of people has lost yet another adult, but it has a new child. And it has new knowledge, a new way of giving birth.

4. Honoring Mother: A BlessingWay Ceremony

Jeannine Parvati Baker

The BlessingWay Ceremony, ancient yet still practiced today, is an organized tour, of great psychological import, through the mysteries

---

Jeannine Parvati Baker is internationally recognized as a midwife and healer. Her book *Hygeia: A Woman's Herbal* is noted as a classic in it's field.

of transition. It is the traditional Navajo way to honor a young woman entering fertility, a pregnant woman about to give birth, or for some other related celebration.

On October 10, 1998, I was inspired to conduct a modified BlessingWay Ceremony to honor the oldest female relative in the family, my mother. With the help of my sister, we gathered the extended family in Sherman Oaks, California for a different kind of reunion, one in which we all sat in a circle, joined by our stories of love and woven together as *One* by a ball of yarn wrapped around each wrist. But I'm getting ahead of myself. First I must recount where the inspiration came from. Before the actual Ceremony could come to be, there had to be a shift, an opening toward healing. Or as the natives say, whatever happens here on Earth must first be dreamed.

I had been talking on the telephone with my sister about our mother's health. She expressed her hope that something would shift as my sister was also having physical problems and found it challenging to care for our mother. As we spoke together, I had a vision. I saw our entire family seated together with our caring ties made apparent. We were enveloped in a circle of love, deep blood love and my mother was hearing those things ordinarily saved for funerals. I thought, why wait to eulogize? Why not hold a ceremony where the family could speak their accolades and personal stories to my mother while she was still alive? My sister didn't know about the Navajo BlessingWay format but she could relate to the intention of the Ceremony. So with her support, we invited family members to gather at my cousin's home in California one lovely Saturday afternoon.

My mother although suffering from problems with her heart and her eyes was in stable, if infirm, health. So there was no urgency to have this honoring ceremony; just my intuition that said better sooner than later. As it turned out, everyone in the extended family came save one nephew in a convalescent hospital and his mother, my mother's youngest and only living sister.

Four of the six of my wonderful children and my Granddaughter came to celebrate the BlessingWay for their beloved Grandmother. Family came from as far away as Utah and Texas. For my youngest three, it was only the idea of honoring Grandma that would coax them from their home after so much traveling this year. We had just returned from Europe then went back to the East Coast a few days before the long drive back to California. Our motivation was BlessingWay; the fuel: love for Grandma!

The Ceremony itself was introduced as having four parts: 1) Showing Up; 2) Focusing on What Has Heart & Meaning; 3) Telling the

Truth; and 4) Being Open Yet Unattached to the Outcome. This was actualized as 1) Song; 2) Wrapping of Yarn/Ritual Grooming; 3) Introductions and Why We Are Here with Gifts; and 4) More Song and Feasting (Potluck).

My mother wanted to sing the lullaby song she used to sing to her babies. I sang it to mine and now her great grand daughter knows it. At the end of the Ceremony, it was my mother who again burst into song, this time show tunes with her brother and nephew, wearing the new T-shirt with the photo of her with her daughters taken 30 years ago.

At the beginning of the Ceremony, many spoke of their love for my mother and by the time it was her turn to wrap the "power object", the ball of yarn around her wrist, she was already weeping in gratitude for all she had heard and felt from our relations. Later my cousin said that this was the most healing day of his life. Indeed, it was over the top with love—all found that precious place of gratitude and a way to share it with each other during and after the ceremony. BlessingWay has the tendency to draw out the beauty in people.

My mother said it best: Though everyone brought gifts for her, each one's presence was "the true gift." It is the Give Away which unites us with love, the ceremony of life.

Post Script:

My mother was called in by her doctor to receive the results of her annual medical exam. The week I wrote this commentary she was 77 years old. Her doctor said that it is rare that he can tell a patient such great news. The hole in her mitral valve had sealed on its own! He is astounded and doesn't know how it happened.

Journal of Prenatal and Perinatal Psychology and Health, 13(3–4), Spring/Summer 1999

BOOK AND VIDEO REVIEWS

The Prenatal Person: Frank Lake's Maternal-Fetal Distress Syndrome, by Stephen M. Maret, Ph.D. (1997). Lanham, MD and Oxford, UK: University Press of America. 218 pages. Hard cover, extensive bibliography. ISBN: 0761807683.

This book examines Frank Lake's Maternal-Fetal Distress Syndrome (M-FDS), as a new and far-reaching paradigm in counseling. The main thesis is that a prenatal environment exists at conception, followed by a week of blissful "union" and non-attachment (the blastocystic stage), then implantation takes place, and a mother-baby bond evolves during pregnancy. The first trimester of intrauterine life is the source of profound imprints affecting one through adult life. Being a physician and an Anglican theologian, Lake's paradigm integrates major sources of knowledge about prenatal development, including physiology, psychology, and theology.

According to Lake, the bi-directional flow of "umbilical affect" between the mother and her unborn baby can result in three relationship patterns based on the *mother's positive, negative, or strongly negative* emotions. The mother's emotions inspire four variations of fetal response which range from the most *"ideal"* state of warm and connected happiness, to good enough *"coping,"* *"opposition,"* (aggressively active to passively non-cooperative), and *"transmarginal stress"* (a catastrophic state in which "the self turns against itself"). Here lie the roots of maternal-fetal distress syndrome, creating a psycho-physiological predisposition toward personality disorders or psychosomatic symptoms. These forces may also complicate pregnancy and giving birth. For Lake, there is also an ontology of the *normal* mother-child relationship, based on two input phases (being/well-being) and two output phases (status/achievement) at each developmental stage. These, in turn, effect the subsequent exchanges.

Lake's method focuses on two areas, (1) the mother's distress during pregnancy which is transferred to the fetus and is accessible via history-taking with the adult, and (2) adult symptoms which can be traced back in "primal integration work." Since prenatal and birth memories are largely unconscious, Lake thought they must be retrieved through methods inducing an altered state comparable to the original state; e.g., via psychedelic drugs, deep breathing, and trance/hypnosis.

Whatever methods are utilized, awareness of the intricate emotional exchanges between mother and fetus facilitates our understanding of adjustment and personality organization in adulthood. Umbilical affect, mediated by the placenta through the umbilical cord, conveys "physical feelings" of aggression or submission, emptiness or fullness, giving and taking, which precede "psychological feelings."

The evidence for M-FDS in Lake's work came in two phases: LSD research (1954–1970), and the primal integration workshops held at Lingdale, England (1975–1982). LSD-25, used in the presence of a trusted therapist, helped patients retrieve disturbing prenatal episodes and birth traumata. Use of LSD-25 was stopped when Lake found out that deep breathing alone (and Reich-inspired bioenergetics) could elicit primal recall.

Lake's primal integration workshops included primal therapy, personal growth, prayer and healing. Over 500 persons attended these workshops at Lingdale (1975–1982), which sometimes lasted a whole week. Once attendees felt "safe" with one another and the instructors, they explored their life history. They also learned about the anatomy and physiology of conception and fetal life. In small groups and in dimly lit rooms, the participants relaxed and were instructed in deep breathing. They then curled up, and "re-created" the sequence of experiences from conception to the first six weeks, and to the first, second, and third trimesters of fetal life. This process included a reenactment of birth. Some participants returned to Lingdale for "re-entry" into their own experiences—with significant therapeutic benefits. The tapes and transcripts from the lengthy Lingdale sessions and a follow-up postal survey of attendees supported Lake's theory of Maternal-Fetal Distress Syndrome.

Lake's insights were shared by other authors, who have produced clinical evidence of birth and prenatal memories in the course of psychoanalysis (O. Rank, S. Fodor, P. Greenacre, D. Fairbanks, M. Klein), "holotropic breathwork" (S. Grof), and hypnosis (D. Cheek, D. Chamberlain). In many instances, primal memories were confirmed by hospital records, parents, and other observers who were present.

Maret shows how Lake created a psychotherapeutic model grounded in theology, drawing upon traditions from Catholicism to Classical Buddhism. Lake made an analogy between the "womb" and "womb of the spirit," postulating derivatives of M-FDS in the psychosomatic complaints of St. John of the Cross, or in Soren Kierkegaard's existential despair, among others. Lake's therapy utilized "communication of God's love, and identification through Christ on the Cross to those suffering pain through no fault of their own." Lake believed that this spiritual dimension lends the ego "supernatural fortitude" to endure the conflicts uncovered through treatment.

Maret comprehensively discusses Lake's theory and practice by reviewing the scientific evidence (anecdotal, clinical, and empirical research) for maternal-fetal distress syndrome. Next, he quotes from Lake's writings on the links between M-FDS and biblical/theological sources, and finally, he presents a contemporary update of empirical research substantiating a psycho-socio-biological view of fetal behavior from the earliest phases of intrauterine life until birth. This impressive section notes recent empirical studies of fetal behavior, including sensations, perceptions, basic emotions, cognitions, and psychophysiological reactions. Maret extols Lake's contribution to pastoral counseling and prenatal psychology with his paradigm integrating science and theology. Not only is M-FDS affirmed in this way, but also the continuity of prenatal, perinatal, and post-natal development.

This book is provocative and intriguing. It presents a thesis which is familiar to students of prenatal development, and to many a psychotherapist who has unexpectedly found primal memories at the core of a patient's pattern of conflicts in the here and now. Maret's approach to looking at the prenatal person is valuable for health professionals, pastoral counselors, and educators and can be a guide to therapists utilizing hypnosis and other techniques for working in an altered state. Maret optimistically predicts that as research technology improves, there will be increasing access to the study of unborn babies, which in turn will shed light on all of psychology.

Susana A. Hassan-Schwarz Galle, Ph.D.
Washington, D.C.

Video Review: *Gentle Touch® Infant Massage* Produced by pediatrician Andrea Gravatt and infant massage instructor Emma Miller (1996), 47 minutes, digitally mastered; $29.95 for individuals, $59.95 for institutions.
Distributed by Gentle Touch, Inc., P.O Box 6007, Asheville, NC 28816, (888 333-3936).

Gentle Touch® Infant Massage, written by APPPAH member Emma Miller, D. Div., and Certified Infant Massage Instructor, is different from other infant massage videos in several ways. What I found most appealing is that the massage demonstrations are done in home environments by parents (two mothers and a father), one at a time, in real time on live babies as opposed to being done in a gymnasium by a massage instructor quickly stroking a doll and remarking to a group of observing mothers, "You will be doing this more slowly at home."

After opening with a simple warning of contraindications, the video begins with an introduction by pediatrician and parent Dr. Olson Huff, Medical Director of the Ruth & Billy Graham Children's Health Center of Mission-St. Joseph's Health System in Asheville, North Carolina. Brief comments by other professionals (including the video's executive producer Dr. Andrea Gravatt) explaining the physical and emotional benefits of infant massage are non-intrusively interspersed throughout the video.

The majority of the video, however, is dedicated to step-by-step massage demonstrations narrated by the parents themselves. The Gentle Touch® technique honors the baby's boundaries and right to be touched by first having the parent ask the infant's permission to perform the massage. The video then shows what verbal and nonverbal cues to look for in the child that communicate her or his readiness to receive your touch. The video also acknowledges the child's right to refuse touch, and clearly demonstrates overstimulation signals as well.

The massage routines are presented progressively (with many close-up camera angles), beginning with simple sustained touch, to broad effleurage strokes and finally focused pettrissage. Another unique element to the *Gentle Touch® Infant Massage* video is that it demonstrates various positions for the parents, since the standard kneeling or sitting cross-legged stances can be uncomfortable for adults with knee problems, even for 15-minute intervals. The video shows parents how to relax their own bodies and spirits first.

Soft music plays throughout the video and parents spontaneously sing nursery rhymes while stroking. It is also a pleasure to hear the babies cooing in response to the massage. The message and tone of the video are further enhanced by the subtitles and quotations about touch such as: "To touch is to give life" and "We need touch just like we need food and water."

For either individual or group instruction, *Gentle Touch® Infant Massage* is the best I have seen for incorporating the medical statistics, demonstrating the stroking techniques, and setting a mood for this special type of infant-parent bonding.

Theresa M. Danna, MPW
Certified Massage Therapist
Encino, California

APPPAH Publications and Tapes

First Congress, Toronto, 1983. Selected papers by Thomas Verny (Ed.), *Pre-& Perinatal Psychology: An Introduction,* New York: Human Sciences Press, 1987.

First Congress casette tapes may be obtained from Herdi Media Ltd., 31 Rail-side Rd., Don Mills, Ontario, M3A 1B2, Canada. Tel. (416) 444-5710.

Second Congress, San Diego, 1985. Tapes of presentations available directly from TDM, Inc., 560 S. State College Blvd., Fullerton, CA 92631.

Third Congress, San Francisco, 1987. Audio casettes of presentations may be obtained from CCC, 37 Indian Rock Rd., San Anselmo, CA 94960.

Fourth Congress, Amherst, MA, 1989; Fifth Congress, Atlanta, GA, 1991; Sixth Congress, Washington, DC, 1993; Seventh Congress and Eigth Congress, San Francisco, CA, 1995, and 1997. Audio casettes of presentations may be obtained from Sounds True, PO Box 8010, Boulder, CO 80306 Tel. (800) 333-9185.

Past Congress Conference Programs and Syllabuses of Abstracts may be purchased from APPPAH headquarters for $5.00 each. Syllabus includes names and addresses of all speakers.

Past issues of The APPPAH Newsletter may be ordered from headquarters for $3 (members) or $5 (non-members) including postage.

Membership in APPPAH includes 1) The *Journal of Prenatal and Perinatal Psychology and Health* 2) The APPPAH Newsletter and 3) the annual revision of *One Hundred Books (and Videos Too)* in Prenatal/Perinatal Psychology and Health.

Copies of the annual revision of *One Hundred Books (and Videos Too)* in Prenatal/Perinatal Psychology and Health may be ordered from headquarters for $5 (members) or $10 (non-members) including postage.

APPPAH Headquarters
340 Colony Road, Box 994
Geyserville, CA 95441-0994
U.S.A.

Telephone: (707) 857-4041
Fax: (707) 857-4042
E-mail: apppah@aol.com

APPPAH Membership Application

Membership dues include the *Journal of Prenatal and Perinatal Psychology and Health* and *APPPAH Newsletter*. Because membership dues barely meet our expenses we ask those who can to make a donation to APPPAH. The suggested amount is one hour's professional fees of any member. In this way, each person may contribute according to his or her means and we can keep our membership accessible to all.

Your membership dues and donations are dedicated to the advancement of pre- and perinatal psychology and the urgent circulation of information and insights from this rapidly expanding field to the general public.

Return to: APPPAH
340 Colony Road, Box 994
Geyserville, CA 95441-0994
U.S.A.

Name _____

Address _____

_____

City _____ State _____

Country _____ Zip/Postal Code _____

Telephone _____ Date _____

Occupation _____

Membership dues are in U.S. Dollars only. The membership extends for one year from the date you join. Membership begins when payment is received.

Dues:

North and South		Credit Card Orders
America	$ 75.00	Acct. No. _____
Student (North and South		Exp. Date _____
America only with copy		Signature _____
of student I.D.)	$ 50.00	
All other countries	$100.00	Please do not send cash.
Donation	$_____	
Total enclosed	$_____	

CHANGING YOUR ADDRESS?

In order to receive your journal without interruption, please complete this Change of Address notice and forward to the Publisher, 60 days in advance, if possible.

Old Address: (PLEASE PRINT)

Name _____

Street _____

City _____

State (or Country) _____

Zip Code _____

New Address: (PLEASE PRINT)

Name _____

Street _____

City _____

State (or Country) _____

Zip Code _____

Date New Address Effective: _____

APPPAH
340 Colony Road, Box 994
Geyserville, CA 95441-0994
U.S.A.